ESSENTIALS

SOCCER SKILLS

igloo

Published in 2008
by Igloo Books Ltd
Cottage Farm,
Sywell,
NN6 0BJ

www.igloo-books.com

Cataloguing in Publication Data information
10 9 8 7 6 5 4 3 2 1

ISBN: 978-1-84817-371-2

Project managed by Metro Media Ltd
Editorial and design management: Adam Phillips
Author: Patrick Morgan
Cover design: Andy Huckle
Text and layout: Andy Huckle and Tom Lynton
Illustrations: Richard Pashley
Picture credits: Photos.com, istock.com, Action Images

Printed and manufactured in China

CONTENTS

INTRODUCTION

Matthews, Pelé, Eusebio, Best, Yashin, Beckenbauer, Charlton, Cruyff, Maradona, Ronaldo, Zidane, Ronaldinho, Rooney – the names of the greatest soccer players in history roll off the tongue so easily.

Throughout the decades, these superstars of the game have thrilled countless millions of fans across the world with their breathtaking skills, goal scoring feats and determination to succeed.

Each of them has something in common too: they all started out in soccer as youngsters who were in love with the game and would play at every opportunity.

Pelé, for most people the greatest player ever to kick a soccer ball, didn't even have a proper ball when

One of the greatest players ever to grace the pitch, it was Pelé from Brazil who first called soccer 'the beautiful game'

he started out. He was often seen in the rundown streets of São Paulo, Brazil, kicking around a sock stuffed with paper, or even a grapefruit. It wasn't until he was given a real

soccer ball on his sixth birthday that Pelé – or Edson Arantes do Nascimento to give him his real name – first felt the touch of leather against his shoes.

All the great players will tell you that their very earliest years were all-important to the way their game developed. The Northern Ireland wing wizard George Best grew up kicking a ball around the back streets of Belfast. Diego Maradona lived in a shanty town in Buenos Aires, Argentina, where he first worked on his truly incredible ball skills.

In fact, it's surprising how many of the world's greatest soccer players did not have access to organized coaching sessions, clubs or leagues when they were young. Luxuries such as qualified coaches and proper pitches, equipment and facilities are very much a feature of the modern age of soccer.

You will probably have access to some form of organized coaching, whether it's through your school, a club or another form of soccer support. So you already have one advantage over some of the great players of yesteryear.

You do share something with those great players, though. It's a fair bet that, since you are reading this book, you are in love with the game of soccer. You love every second you spend kicking a ball around, or practicing your goalkeeping saves.

Many of the world's greatest soccer players didn't start on a proper pitch – they had to improvise

Remember – soccer is a game and you should have fun with it!

A love of the game has been the driving force behind many a great soccer career. Once you've started playing soccer, it's often very hard to stop – just ask any retired pro player how difficult it was for them to bow out of the beautiful game. You will share something else in common with these giants of soccer, too – your eagerness to learn. No one ever got anywhere in soccer without listening to their coaches, or without working hard on learning the essential techniques needed to truly excel on the pitch.

Someone once said that genius consists of 99 percent perspiration and one percent inspiration. That means that you'll have to do a lot of sweating before you become a truly great player.

But never forget that soccer is a game, and a game is supposed to be fun. Too many coaches in the past have focused on the hard work of making great players, forgetting to inject some fun into the proceedings. After all, if you're not enjoying your soccer, what's the point in playing it at all?

The aim of this book is to show you the best ways of becoming a better player – but also to make sure you actually enjoy yourself!

Chapter one kicks off with the buzzwords and jargon of soccer. How do you nutmeg an opponent? What is a 'give-and-go pass'? What is the job of a sweeper? Which players would you expect to see overlapping? All these terms and many more are fully explained.

If you really want to get a handle on soccer, you will also need to understand its laws. Chapter two will explain when you are likely to be penalized for being in an offside position; why the referee will blow his whistle for a foul; when the ball is in and out of play; what you can and can't take on to the pitch; and much, much more.

Chapter three will take you through exactly what equipment you will require, and why it's needed.

Then we'll be helping you work out which position best suits you on the pitch. Where do you fit in best in your soccer team? Some top players can play in any position, but it's likely that you'll be better at some soccer roles than others. Chapter four examines every position and looks at the qualities that are needed for each of them.

Chapter five looks at the various systems of play and formations that soccer coaches use. Should your team play in a conventional 4-4-2, use a sweeper in a 1-4-3-2, or opt for a 5-3-2 formation? All will soon be revealed.

In chapter six, we get down to the nitty-gritty of the techniques you will need to enjoy your soccer. These range from controlling the ball to passing, dribbling and heading. Learn such techniques properly and you will shine on the pitch.

And the best place to learn such techniques is during training, which is profiled in chapter seven. With our drills and games aimed at improving your skills, you should end up having a lot of fun during practice as well!

To get the very most out of your soccer, you'll also need to be physically and mentally fit. Chapter eight shows how you should look after yourself on and off the pitch.

Finally, we lift the veil on the history of soccer in chapter nine – from its earliest beginnings in China two thousand years ago through to the modern day World Cup.

The humble grapefruit is one of the items Pelé learnt to play soccer with

NAME OF THE GAME

Here are all the pieces of terminology and jargon you're likely to hear when playing soccer. Bear in mind that we're leaving out the terms that are explained in the laws of the game, as these will be covered in the next chapter.

Needless to say, the language of the game is changing all the time, and new words and phrases enter the vocabulary every year. However, what follows will give you a good grounding in soccer-speak.

No matter how young or old, a player should always listen to their coach because the coach will know all soccer's jargon off by heart!

The substitutes sit on the bench waiting to be called into action

Advantage: Sequence of play in which the referee allows play to continue after an infringement of the law if it benefits the team against which the foul has been committed.

Assist: Pass that leads to a goal.

Attack: Players who are mainly responsible for creating and scoring goals.

Attacker or striker: Player who plays in the attack and whose main duty is to score goals.

Away: Instruction to teammate to clear the ball.

Back and face: Instruction to players to drop back and face the play.

Back door: Instruction to teammate to pass the ball behind him.

Back heel: Backwards pass or shot using the heel.

Back pass: A pass backwards, usually to the goalkeeper. The keeper may not handle a back pass if it has been made with a foot.

Ball watching: Mistake made by defenders who concentrate on the movement of the ball rather than their opponents.

Bench: An area outside the pitch used by coaches, medical people and substitutes to view the soccer game.

Bend: Make a ball curve in the air by striking it on one of its sides, with either the inside or the outside of the foot.

WHAT IS A BANANA KICK?

Look at the shape of a banana and it'll give you a clue to the path of a banana kick through the air. The ball is 'bent' by the kicker, causing it to curve in the air. It's a skill that takes a lot of practice to master.

You'll need to strike the ball on one of its sides with either the inside or outside of your foot.

The great Brazilian sides of the 50s and 60s were among the first to show off their banana kick prowess, and that tradition is carried on in the modern game by Real Madrid's attacking left back Roberto Carlos.

For inspiration, watch Roberto's amazing free kick against France in 1997, or check out the master of banana kicks, David Beckham!

The humble banana inspired soccer players to come up with a kick that bends through the air

Bicycle kick or scissor kick: Backwards pass or shot for which the player leaps and, while upside-down in the air, kicks the ball when it is directly above him.

Booking: Caution given by the referee, usually signalled by a yellow card.

Break or breakaway: Fast movement of the ball from defense to attack, sometimes while opposing players are committed upfield.

Center back, central defender or stopper: Defender who occupies the middle area of the defensive line.

Center forward: Attacker who is often the pivotal point of a team's attacking play.

Channel: Space between defenders into which a ball can be passed for an attacker to run on to.

Chip: A soft, high pass or shot made by striking the lower part of the ball.

Clear: Remove the ball from a danger area.

Close down: Put an opponent under pressure by denying them space.

Create space: Move out of an area of the field, with opponents following. The space which has been freed up can then be used by teammates.

Cross or center: Attacking pass from a wing into the middle of the field.

Dead ball: Restart of play with a stationary ball, such as a corner kick or free kick.

England's formidable striker Michael Owen demonstrates the power of a scissor kick. It's one of the most difficult moves to master, but remains one of the most impressive and devastating!

Defender: Player who is positioned in front of the goalkeeper and whose first duty is to limit the number of scoring opportunities available to opponents.

Defense: Unit of the team whose main responsibility is defending their own goal at all costs.

Dribble: Run with the ball under close control by the feet.

Far post or back post: The goalpost furthest from the position of the ball.

Fifty-fifty ball: Loose ball contested by two players, each of whom has an equal chance of winning the challenge.

Finish: Score a goal.

Flat back four: Defensive system using four defenders.

Forwards: Attackers who occupy the most forward positions.

Full back: Defender who is usually responsible for a wide position.

Futsal: The name for indoor soccer.

Goalkeeper, **goalie**, **keeper or goaltender:** Player who may handle the ball inside the penalty area and whose first responsibility is to stop goals being scored.

The goalkeeper's job is a tough one – especially when they end up with a ball in the back of their net

Half-time: Interval between the two periods of play in a match.

Half-volley: Pass, shot or clearance in which a dropping ball is struck by the foot as it touches the ground.

Hat-trick: Feat of scoring three goals in a match.

Header: Passing, clearing or shooting with the head

Inswinger: Cross or corner kick that curves towards the goal.

Jockey: Confront and contain an opponent without tackling them for the ball.

Kick-off: Start of play (or restart after a goal has been scored) at which the ball is played from the center spot.

Long ball: Long pass aimed at a forward or advanced area of the field.

A good opening kick-off can set the tone for the rest of the game

This is what happens when a player realizes he has scored an own goal...

Man on: Warning to a teammate that an opponent is approaching him.

Mark: Take on defensive responsibility for an opposing player by staying close to them.

Midfield: The area between defense and attack. Midfield players form the link between defenders and attackers.

Near post: The goal post nearest to the position of the ball.

Nutmeg: Beat a defender by knocking the ball between their legs and running round them to continue your run.

Offside trap: Tactic used to leave opponents in an offside position.

One-two, give-and-go or wall pass: Passing sequence in which a player passes to a teammate and then runs straight into a space to receive an immediate return pass.

Outswinger: Cross or corner kick that curves deliberately away from the goal.

Overlap: Run past a teammate, usually on a wing, to receive a pass or create space.

Own goal: Goal scored by a player in the goal they are defending.

Pass: Deliver the ball to a teammate.

Penalty area, penalty box, 18-yard area or 18-yard box: The area in which a goalkeeper may handle the ball and in which a foul is punished by a penalty kick. Sometimes also called the 'big box' or 'box'.

Pick up: Move to within marking distance of an opponent.

Playmaker: Midfield player around which much of the attacking play revolves.

Save: Catch, parry or deflection by the goalkeeper that prevents a goal being scored.

Sending off: The ejection from the field of play of a player who has received a red card.

Set piece: Restart such as a free kick or corner kick that has been planned and rehearsed.

Shin guards or shin pads: Equipment made from rubber, plastic or a similar substance worn under the stockings ('socks' in the UK) to protect the shins.

Short corner: Short pass at a corner kick.

Shot: Attempt at a goal.

Six-yard-box, six-yard-area, goal box or goal area: Rectangular area in front of each goal. The line parallel with the goal line is where goal kicks are taken from. Sometimes also called the 'small box'.

Slide tackle: Tackle in which a player slides in horizontally to take the ball from an opponent.

Square pass or square ball: A pass played to a teammate who is parallel to or behind the passer.

Sub: Short term for substitute.

Switch play: Pass the ball from one side of the pitch to the other.

A coach watches anxiously from the sidelines of the pitch as he sends on two of his substitutes

WHAT DOES A SWEEPER DO?

Pictured here is Franz Beckenbauer, one of the world's greatest ever sweepers

The sweeper, sometimes called the libero, is a defender who, in some team formations, plays behind the main defensive line but in front of the goalkeeper.

Their job is to 'sweep' up behind the defensive line to protect the goal-keeper from any of the opponents' attacking play that threatens to develop into a scoring chance.

One of the greatest sweepers of all time was Franz Beckenbauer, the German soccer legend who was a World Cup winner twice over – once as a player and once as a coach.

Some formations have a sweeper or libero in front of a back four, and 'libero' can also sometimes mean a player who is given the license to roam wherever they want to on the field.

Tackle: Dispossess an opponent of the ball by fair means.

Through ball: Pass behind or through a defense for a teammate to run on to.

Trap: Control the ball using the underside of the foot.

Turn: Advice to a teammate that they have time and space to turn with the ball.

Two-footed: Able to kick equally well with either foot.

Volley: Pass, shoot or clear by kicking the ball while it is in the air.

Wall: Defensive line of players used to shield part of the goal being defended at a free kick.

Wide: The wing or flank areas of the pitch.

Wing or flank: The areas of the pitch nearest the touchlines.

Winger, wide midfielder or wide player: The player who is positioned in the wide areas.

When tackling your opposite man, make sure you keep it clean and legal or you risk incurring the wrath of the referee

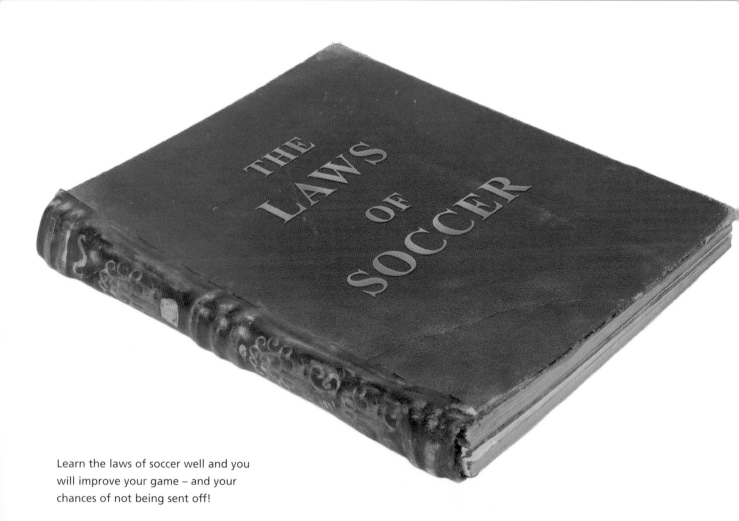

Learn the laws of soccer well and you will improve your game – and your chances of not being sent off!

LETTER OF THE LAW

If you want to enjoy your soccer as much as you possibly can, you need to know, understand and comply with the rules of the game. And your first lesson is to learn to call them 'laws', not rules. Ever since the fateful first meeting of the Football Association way back in 1863, when the way the sport should be played was finally laid down, the correct term has been 'laws'.

From watching TV or matches in your local park, you'll know that the laws of soccer are enforced by a referee, two assistant refs and, sometimes, a fourth official, who stands outside the field of play. They're there to ensure the game is played in a fair manner – and they need the co-operation of all the players on the pitch to carry out their job. That means no cheating, no trying to con the officials and, just as importantly,

no disrespect. Even if you don't agree with the referee's decision – and let's face it, it's sometimes hard to see the reasoning behind some decisions – it's your duty to your teammates and coach not to dispute it.

The referee is not about to change his mind, and you run the risk of being disciplined or even expelled from the field of play for sounding off!

THE FIELD OF PLAY AND THE BALL

The laws say the field must be rectangular, with a minimum length of 295ft/90m, a maximum length of 394ft/120m, a minimum width of 148ft/45m and a maximum width of 295ft/90m. The field is divided into two by a halfway line, with a center mark at its midpoint and a 30ft/9.15m-radius circle marked out around it. The two long boundaries are touch lines and the shorter ones are goal lines. Penalty marks are painted 38ft/11m from each goal.

There are goal areas (marked out 18ft/5.5m from the goals) at each end and penalty areas (marked out 54ft/16.5m from the goals) outside them. The goals are made up of two white goalposts (maximum 5.7in/12cm width and depth) 24ft/7.32m apart and a crossbar, which is 8ft/2.44m from the ground.

At each corner of the field, an arc with a radius of 3.3ft/1m is painted,

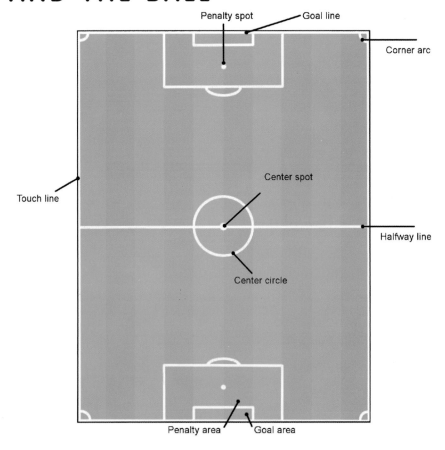

Penalty spot

Goal line

Corner arc

Touch line

Center spot

Halfway line

Center circle

Penalty area

Goal area

and flagposts are normally placed at each corner. What about the ball? It must be spherical, made of leather or a similar material and not more than 28in/70cm in circumference. It must not weigh more than 450g.

While we're talking figures, let's cover the duration of a match, which is normally 90 minutes, split into two equal halves of 45 minutes. However, junior soccer matches are often shorter affairs and that's fine as long as the length of play is agreed by the two teams and the referee beforehand.

The referee makes allowances for time lost through such events as substitutions, injuries to players and time-wasting. If a penalty kick is being taken when the end of the match arrives, play is extended until the kick is completed. Half-time intervals may not exceed more than 15 minutes.

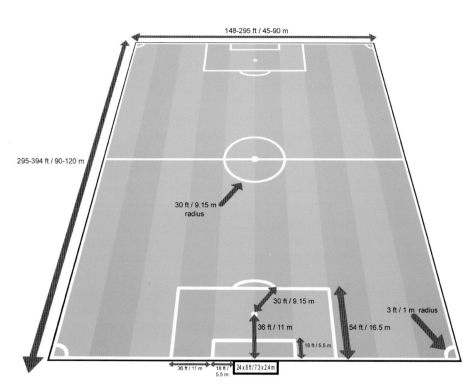

148-295 ft / 45-90 m

295-394 ft / 90-120 m

30 ft / 9.15 m radius

30 ft / 9.15 m

36 ft / 11 m

3 ft / 1 m radius

54 ft / 16.5 m

18 ft / 5.5 m

36 ft / 11 m

18 ft / 5.5 m

24 x 8 ft / 7.3 x 2.4 m

Shown here are the areas and dimensions of the modern soccer pitch – if you practice hard enough, one day you could find yourself playing on one of these...

PLAYERS AND THEIR EQUIPMENT

The laws say no 11-a-side match can start or continue if either team has fewer than seven players. The number of substitutes can vary, depending on what kind of match or tournament your team is playing in, but usually the maximum number of subs is three. The subs' names must be given to the referee before the match, and substitutes must not enter the field of play without the ref's permission.

That goes for all players, in fact. You may not leave or enter the field of play unless the referee says you can

– and no player may change places with their goalkeeper without the ref giving it the okay. When it comes to equipment, safety is all-important, and you're not allowed to use or wear anything that might be dangerous to yourself or another player – this includes any kind of jewelry or piercings.

You must wear a jersey or shirt with sleeves, shorts, stockings, shin-guards (covered fully by the stockings) and footwear. Goalkeepers must wear different colors from the other players and the officials.

Your soccer uniform has its own set of regulations that must be adhered to

THE REFEREE AND ASSISTANT REFEREES

The duties of the referee are many, but the main ones are to enforce the laws, control the match with the help of the assistant referees and, if necessary, to take disciplinary action against those players he believes deserve to be cautioned or – even worse – sent off.

Don't forget, the referee's decision is final, so there's no point trying to influence him after he's made his mind up. The only time he can change it is when he realizes it's incorrect or if an assistant referee advises that it's incorrect.

The assistant referees are there to help the referee make decisions on a multitude of issues.

These include such instances as when the ball has left the field of play; which team should have a corner kick, goal kick or throw-in; when a player may be penalized for being in an offside position; when something of which the referee should be aware has happened out of his view; and when offences have been committed closer to the assistant than to the referee himself.

Assistant referees are not always popular with players but they serve an invaluable role

STARTING AND RESTARTING PLAY

Once a coin has been flipped and the winner has decided which goal their side will attack in the first half, it's time for the other team to kick off – and this also happens when a goal has been scored and at the start of the second half. All players should be in their own half and opposing players outside the center circle.

The ball is kicked forward from the center spot when the referee signals, and the kicker may not touch it again until it has been touched by another player.

Another way of restarting play, after a temporary stoppage (an injury, for example), is the dropped ball. The ref drops the ball at the place where it was when play was stopped.

When the referee blows that whistle at kick-off, you know that anything could happen in the next 90 minutes – that is what's so magical about soccer

BALL OUT OF PLAY AND SCORING GOALS

There are two answers to the question: 'When is the ball out of play?' One is when play has been stopped by the referee; the other is when the ball has entirely crossed the goal line or touch line (and entirely means entirely; even if a tiny portion of the ball is level with the line, it's not out of play).

It's a similar situation when it comes to scoring a goal. The whole of the ball has to pass over the whole of the goal line – between the goal posts and under the crossbar, naturally – for the goal to count. And, for the referee to mark down the goal, he has to be satisfied that no offense was committed by the scoring team.

When the ball is out of play it will require a throw-in from one of the players to get the game started again

OFFSIDE

This is the most controversial law in soccer, causing debate and argument after every match, it sometimes seems. It's probably also the least understood law. First, it's important to know that it's not an offense for players to be in an offside position, and that there's no offense if they receive the ball directly from a goal kick, throw-in or corner kick.

Next, you need to know when a player is actually in an offside position, and it's fairly simple: when they are nearer to the opponents' goal line than the ball and the second to last opponent.

Players are not in an offside position if they are in their own half of the field, are level with the second to last opponent, or are level with the last two opponents.

But a player in an offside position can only be penalized if, at the very moment the ball is touched or is played by a teammate, he is, in the referee's opinion, still involved in active play.

What does 'involved in active play' mean? It has three possible meanings: interfering with play; interfering with an opponent; or gaining an advantage by being in that position.

It all sounds quite complex, but in fact the offside law is fairly simple. Remember, it's always the referee's opinion that counts, not yours or your coach's.

When the ref is sure an offside offense has been committed, he awards an indirect free kick to the opposing team.

If you see this flag then you may as well stop your run on the goal because you're offside!

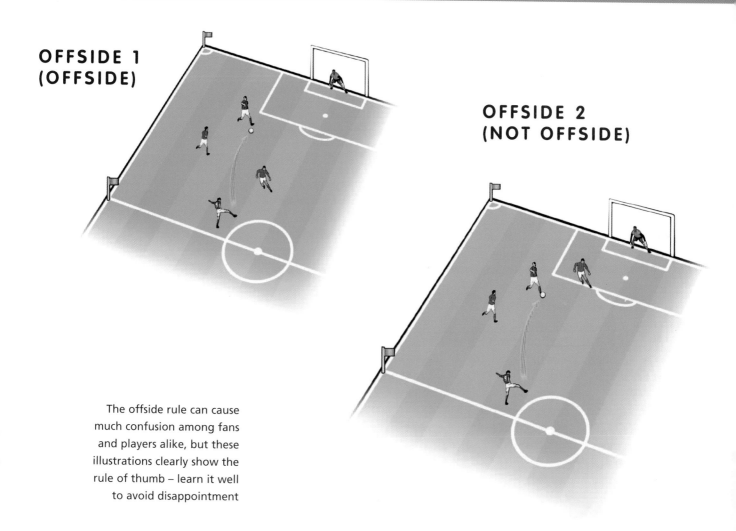

**OFFSIDE 1
(OFFSIDE)**

**OFFSIDE 2
(NOT OFFSIDE)**

The offside rule can cause
much confusion among fans
and players alike, but these
illustrations clearly show the
rule of thumb – learn it well
to avoid disappointment

FREE KICKS

There are two types of free kick: direct and indirect. First, indirect, and we've already seen that one of these is awarded if an offside offense takes place. The referee also awards an indirect free kick if a player plays in a dangerous manner, impedes the progress of an opposing player or stops the goalkeeper releasing the ball from his hands.

There are more indirect free kick offenses: if a goalkeeper takes more than six seconds to release the ball from his hands; if he touches it again with his hands after releasing it, provided it hasn't touched another player; and if the goalkeeper touches the ball with his hands after it has been deliberately kicked or thrown to him by a teammate. Let's move on to direct free kicks, which will be awarded if any of these offenses has been committed:

● Kicking, attempting to kick, tripping or attempting to trip an opposing player.
● Jumping or charging at an opposing player.
● Striking, attempting to strike or pushing an opponent.
● Tackling an opponent and making contact with them before touching the ball.
● Holding an opponent.
● Spitting at an opponent.
● Handling the ball deliberately – except for the goalkeeper inside his own penalty area.

If any of the above offenses are committed inside a penalty area, the referee awards a penalty kick.

A free kick can turn a game around for a losing side – so be sure not to give the ref any excuse to award one to the opposing team!

PENALTY KICKS

There are simple rules governing penalty kicks, which are taken from the penalty mark:

● The defending goalkeeper must stay on his goal line, between the goalposts, facing his opponent until the ball has been kicked.

● All players except the kicker and the goalkeeper must be outside the penalty area, behind the penalty mark and at least 30ft/9.15m from the penalty mark.

● The kicker may not touch the ball a second time until it has been touched by another player.

No one wants a soccer match to end in a penalty shoot-out, but sometimes it's necessary

PROCEED WITH CAUTION!

The dreaded yellow and red cards – signifying a caution and a sending-off respectively – are a fairly recent introduction to soccer, but they've made the work of the referee easier and helped spectators understand what's happening.

The referee *will* caution a player if that player:

● Is guilty of unsporting behavior.

● Shows dissent.

● Persistently infringes the laws.

● Delays the restart of play.

● Fails to respect the 30ft/9.15m distance limit at corner kicks and free kicks.

● Enters or re-enters the field, or leaves the field deliberately, without the referee giving permission.

And the official *will* send off a player if that player:

● Is guilty of serious foul play or violent conduct.

● Spits at an opponent or anyone else.

● Denies the opponents a goal or obvious goal-scoring opportunity by handling the ball.

● Denies an opponent an obvious goalscoring opportunity by committing an offense punishable by a free kick or penalty kick.

● Uses offensive, insulting or abusive language.

● Receives a second caution in a match.

The red card – if the referee shows
you one of these, it's game over

THROW-INS, GOAL KICKS AND CORNER KICKS

Throw-ins, goal kicks and corner kicks all offer excellent chances for tipping the game in your team's favor

These are all ways of restarting play when the ball has crossed one of the boundary lines.

For a throw-in, the thrower faces the field of play, with part of each foot on the touch line or outside it, and throws the ball from behind and over his head using both hands. No player may be within 6.6ft/2m of the point at which the throw-in is taken, and the thrower may not touch the ball again until it has been touched by at least one other player.

A goal kick is awarded when the ball crosses a goal line having been touched last by a member of the attacking team – and not between the goalposts! To take a goal kick, any member of the defending team kicks the ball from any point within the goal area, while the opponents stay outside the penalty area. The ball is in play when it has passed outside the penalty area, and the kicker may not touch it again until another player has touched it.

A corner kick is the result of the ball crossing a goal line having been touched last by a member of the defending team. The ball is placed inside the corner arc at the nearest corner and is kicked by an attacking player. Opponents must stay 30ft/9.15m away until the ball is back in play – when it has moved, in other words.

These are the essential laws of the game of soccer, although there is much more to learn about control of the game. If you're serious about soccer, it would be worth visiting a bookstore to buy a copy of the laws to educate yourself fully on all aspects of the 'beautiful' game.

Make that throw-in count!

GOING EQUIPPED

Being successful at soccer, or even just having fun, is not simply a matter of learning all the techniques and skills and then putting them into practice. It's also a question of having the correct equipment, whether it's the very basic stuff such as clothing and a ball, or less obvious equipment that is used for safety reasons.

Then there's the equipment that's needed for a successful and enjoyable coaching session, like cones and bibs. Let's start our chapter on soccer equipment with a look at something without which no match or coaching session could start.

The locker room is where last-minute winning strategies can be planned

THE BALL

Choose your weapon: have a ball handy at all times

As we've already seen, the laws of soccer state that the ball must be spherical, made of leather or another suitable material and must not be more than 28in/70cm in circumference or weigh more than 450g. Also, the pressure of the match ball has to be equal to 600 to 1,100 grams per square centimeter – this is something your coach and refs will be able to check. The ball should be firm, but an adult should be able to press into it slightly with their thumb.

Well, those are the regulations for the adult game, but experts recommend that children up to the age of 10 should use a slightly smaller, size 4 ball. Even younger kids will use a size 3 but

the day will come when you'll progress to the full-size 5 ball.

The days of leather footballs that soaked up water and got heavier as a match went on, until kicking it was like kicking a cannonball, are long gone, and today's ball has a waterproof surface so its weight remains pretty much constant.

CLEATS (OR BOOTS)

All sports equipment manufacturers spend millions of dollars every year trying to get the design of their soccer footwear right for today's players – and some stars are paid big money to wear the boots they produce.

The soccer cleats (called boots or shoes in the UK) of today are slim, lightweight affairs compared to the heavy, rugged footwear of days gone by. Players find the modern style gives them better control over the ball, and some designers go to great lengths to produce cleats that look good at the same time as giving a player an advantage over opponents.

But you should be aware that comfort and the protection your cleats give your feet are more important than the way they look. You're going to be doing a lot of running, jumping, kicking and tackling in your new footwear so, before you or your parents decide on a pair, make sure they're right for you.

Many leagues have rules about the type of footwear you can wear during a match, and it's vital that your cleats do not endanger your teammates or opponents in any way. Modern soccer cleats have all kinds of structures on their soles, and it's up to you, your coach and the referee to make sure they're not dangerous to wear.

The modern soccer cleat is a masterclass in cutting-edge design, but you don't have to spend a fortune to buy a pair of cleats that's right for you

SHINGUARDS

FIFA's laws of soccer make it clear that shinguards must be worn during a match and, besides, it's plain common sense to wear them. They can prevent nasty, very painful and sometimes dangerous lower leg injuries, which nevertheless can be pretty common in soccer. After ankle and knee injuries, they're the problems that occur most often in the sport.

The laws also state that your shinguards must be covered entirely by your stockings; that they must be made of a suitable material like rubber, plastic or a similar substance; and that they must provide a reasonable degree of protection.

As with footwear, it's worth trying on a few shinguards in your local sports store to find out what suits you best. And, while you're there, make sure that the pair you choose gives protection to your ankles as well as your shins.

Your lower legs are at risk of injury during tackling, so shin guards are an absolute must

GOALKEEPERS' GLOVES

These are another piece of soccer equipment that should be tried on before you buy them, so that rules out mail order and internet buying. A goalie's gloves will probably be his most treasured soccer possession, and a good pair will last a long time.

Make sure they're a good fit, they give your hands some protection and don't limit your

The right gloves can make all the difference when catching a ball as it heads towards you

MOUTH GUARDS

Think about it: how many collisions between players do you see in the average match? And how many times do you see a player receive a ball full in the face? The answer to both questions is 'quite a few', and when you consider how much care you take of your mouth and teeth off the soccer field, you realize it makes complete sense to think about wearing a mouth guard.

Essential for protecting your teeth while on the pitch

ability to catch, deflect or parry the ball. If you can, try punching a ball with them before you buy, so you know they are right.

Again, it's not important that your gloves look good – it's far more important that they do the job they're meant to do.

The truth is that, in the past, few pro soccer players used mouth guards – but when you see the gaps in their teeth that have resulted from collisions and ball-in-face incidents, you wonder why they didn't. It's not uncommon to see a player spitting out teeth as he gets up from one of these events.

So wear a mouth guard. Okay, it might not be the easiest piece of soccer equipment to get used to, and it might not look great, but it looks better than a black hole where your teeth should be. The humble mouth guard can even be fun because they are available in all kinds of colors and patterns.

UNIFORMS

Uniforms, or strips as they're known in the UK, are used by most teams, and certainly by those that play in organized competitions. Some of the color schemes and designs available to the 21st-century soccer team are stunning, so it's worth getting involved if your team is choosing a new uniform.

The uniform you end up choosing will consist of jerseys, shorts and stockings – and the laws of the game have something to say on these items of clothing.

FIFA says that if a player chooses to wear thermal undershorts (cycle shorts), they must be of the same color as the shorts. If your team has a multicolored uniform, the undershorts must be the same color as the predominant color in the shorts.

Jerseys must have sleeves, says FIFA, and it also points out, of course, that goalkeepers must wear colors that mark them out from the other players and the officials on the pitch.

There are strict guidelines that must be followed to ensure uniforms are just that – uniforms!

FIRST AID KITS

While it would be asking a lot for soccer players to carry a first aid kit wherever they go in case they get involved in a kick-about in the local park, no coaching session or match should start without one.

This is really the responsibility of your coach or whoever is in charge of your team, but it would do no harm for you to make yourself familiar with a standard soccer first aid kit and how to use its contents.

The kit should include bandages for strapping and protecting injuries, and scissors for cutting them; ice packs; antiseptic wipes for treating cuts; a CPR (cardiopulmonary resuscitation) mouth barrier in case a player needs to be resuscitated; a pair of latex gloves for use while

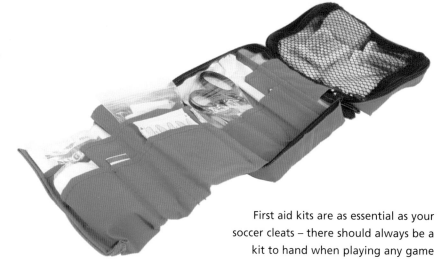

First aid kits are as essential as your soccer cleats – there should always be a kit to hand when playing any game

tending bloody injuries; and a pair of tweezers.

Your coach or medics might also want to add items like insect repellent, sunscreen, eyewash and a tooth-preserving system, in case a player loses a tooth or two. It's a good idea, in any case, to use sunscreen before and maybe during any soccer activity, but especially if you're training or playing in the middle of the day.

WATER

Soccer matches can last a long time and players have been known to get dehydrated, which can be extremely dangerous. At the very least, you won't be performing to the best of your ability if your body is in real need of water.

Don't forget, either, that it's not only in very warm weather that you run the risk of dehydrating, although hot conditions increase the risks.

Unless water bottles are provided by your coach or team organizer, always take one with you to practice sessions or matches, and make sure you will be able to refill it if needed. The key here is little and often: drink a little water as often as you can. You'll be amazed at the real difference it can make.

It's important to keep yourself hydrated during matches

TRAINING EQUIPMENT

No coach would feel complete without his training cones: those orange or red objects that decorate the highways and soccer training sessions of the world. They're used to mark out the areas or distances the coach wants the players to use in a drill.

Training bibs might also be handy in a coaching session, when the coach wants to divide the players into two small-sided teams wearing different-colored tops.

OTHER ISSUES

Some girls mature earlier than others, and those that do will require a sports bra, which needs to be fitted properly. Ask your mother or a female relative to accompany you.

Likewise, some boys will need to wear a protective cup to guard their most vulnerable areas. Good sports stores stock them and will be happy to discuss your needs.

Cones and bibs are ideal for making the most of your practice sessions

Girls need the right equipment to offer support during games

POSITIONAL SENSE

Once you've equipped yourself with the right kit for the job and then taken your first few steps on to the soccer field, you will probably want to start thinking hard about what position you want to play in during a game.

It's a fair bet that most new soccer players will want to play where the glory is – in an attacking position where you can score the goals and gain the admiration of your friends, coach and parents. But there are several things to think about, besides which position you enjoy most, before you decide what's best for you – and your coach may well have a few ideas on the matter, too.

What are your strengths – speed, agility, dribbling ability, good ball control, heading technique, strength in the tackle or perhaps stamina? Which position might be best suited to the way you are built?

There are some notable exceptions, but most goalkeepers are tall, for example. Are you left- or right-footed, or are you equally comfortable kicking with either foot? Do you find it easiest to tackle, to pass or to shoot?

In this chapter, we are going to examine each of the positions in a soccer team (they vary depending on which formation the team plays in, but some positions are constant) and try to help you and your coach decide where you'll fit in best.

The idea of being a striker may be very appealing, but keep an open mind about the other positions available – your skills might suit them better

The goalkeeper is the most specialized player on the field

GOALKEEPER

Call the goalkeeper what you like – goalie, keeper, netminder – they are the most specialized players on the field.

It's often said that to be a goalkeeper you have to be a little crazy. What is certain is that, if you want to be a goalie, you will have to be brave enough to dive at the feet of opponents to scoop up the ball and have absolutely no fear when you go for a high ball in a crowded penalty area.

The goalkeeper is the last line of defense and the first line of offense (or attack, as it's called in the UK). Soccer is a team game but often it becomes a one-on-one between the goalie and an attacker. When outfield players make an error, it often goes unnoticed; when the goalkeeper makes an error, it sometimes means the match will be lost.

So, as well as bravery, a keeper needs a certain amount of mental strength to deal with disappointments. What other qualities must they possess?

You will certainly have to be agile, with the ability to move your feet quickly, for nimble footwork is the start of good goalkeeping. You will also need to have good hand-to-eye co-ordination, meaning you'll be good at catching a ball – and gathering the ball safely, in various ways, will form the basis of a lot of your coaching sessions. A good goalkeeper also knows the importance of concentration and focus. There may be long periods of a match when you're not involved in the play, but let your attention wander at your peril!

Then there's the importance of communicating with defenders. Having a good loud voice and using it to tell them what you intend to do, or what you want them to do, is a big asset – but it's something you can work on!

It will also be handy if you have strong legs, with the ability to send a dead ball a good distance during goal kicks. Again, this is something that can be improved as you progress in the game, and some defenders take goal kicks on behalf of their goalkeepers.

SWEEPER OR LIBERO

Not all playing formations use a sweeper, but it's a very popular position in a lot of countries, and many junior soccer teams employ one. The sweeper is the last line of defense in front of the goal-keeper, and his or her job is to 'sweep up' any errors made or gaps left by the defensive line, and get the ball away from the danger area. But sweepers can have other duties and chances to shine. They're not given defensive marking responsibilities, so they sometimes get the chance to roam upfield, with or without the ball, to pose problems to the opposing defense.

That said, sweepers spend much of the match in the central defensive areas, rarely venturing out to the flanks. They can be the first to start an attack and the last to stub the opponents' offensive moves. Size and stature are not of great importance in this position.

What qualities do you need to be a good sweeper? Certainly the ability to 'read' the game and to understand where offensive threats are coming from, although that skill will only come with experience and a lot of practice.

Sweepers also need to be fast on their feet, for they may have to cover a lot of ground very quickly, and they must be firm and decisive in the tackle.

If you're a good communicator you may well be a good sweeper, and the best liberos are confident people, able to make decisions fast and act on them with firmness.

Good ball control and passing and dribbling ability are valuable pluses in this position and, if you show enough promise, your coach will be delighted to work on these areas with you. A good sweeper is a priceless asset to a team.

Sweepers need to be very
fast on their feet

CENTRAL DEFENDER OR STOPPER

Sometimes known as center backs, these defenders often operate in pairs, occupying the central area of the defensive line and dealing head on with the threat from the opposing team's attackers.

Central defenders seldom have any offensive duties, although they may add to the offensive threat during set pieces like free kicks and corner kicks. Instead, their job is marking the opponents' central attackers or strikers and battling to dispossess them of the ball, whether it's on the ground or in the air.

To be a central defender requires discipline and and decisiveness – both skills shown here by Kolo Toure (left) who plays for UK club Arsenal

Starting off offensive moves, however, is also one of the central defender's duties, although there are times when a hefty boot, sending the ball over the touch line or way upfield, is more effective and valuable than playing it skilfully and carefully out of defense.

In teams playing without a sweeper, the central defenders form the last line of defense before the goalkeeper. It is important that they keep in constant communication with each other.

So, the qualities needed for a good central defender are many. First of all, you will need to be brave if you are to confront attackers in situations that can sometimes be very physically demanding.

Next, you will have to be physically and mentally strong, and be able to move fast across the ground to keep pace with those speedy strikers, or to ensure you are first to the ball. You will also be decisive and disciplined.

Your tackling ability will of course be very important, and you will need to put in a lot of practice at heading the ball. Your ball control and passing ability will be tested when it comes to setting up offensive play.

The soccer field will be one of very few places where you will earn praise for showing aggressiveness. Just don't let that aggressiveness spill over into foul play.

FULL BACK

On either side of the central defenders are the full backs, who are responsible for covering the space on the flanks and marking the opposing team's wingers.

These players aim to cut out the service of the ball from those wingers and other players on the flanks into the center, where the strikers will be waiting to convert the crosses into goals with their heads or feet.

The full backs are in constant communication with their goalkeeper and fellow defenders, aiming to keep the defensive unit tight and in shape.

But they can have their share of offensive duties too. Coaches often want their full backs to raid upfield on the flanks, sometimes overlapping their wingers and central midfield players, with the aim of crossing the ball into the penalty area or helping teammates to do so.

In fact, some team formations dispense with full backs and make use of wing backs, who play as both defenders and attackers, as the situation demands. These players need to be equally comfortable defending and attacking.

Again, the qualities required of full backs are many. They need to be quick and have the stamina to keep running up and down the flanks for the entire game. Full backs should be tough in the tackle but disciplined enough to hold an opposing player in one place rather than rush into a reckless challenge that will give the opponent an unnecessary advantage.

A full back should also be comfortable with the ball at their feet, a good passer and a good crosser of the ball.

It's usually an advantage for a right full back to be right-footed and a left full back to be left-footed, although there are many cases where players have had long professional careers seemingly playing 'out of position'.

Full backs need to be tough, disciplined and good communicators

CENTRAL MIDFIELDER

These players, who often play as a pair in the central areas of the field, are sometimes called the 'engine room' of the team. They're the ones who create, organize and prompt a team's offensive play while also performing defensive duties when they're needed. Some teams will have defensive and offensive specialists in the midfield, sometimes with the defensive player operating just in front of the defensive line; others will ask their central midfielders to play both roles.

A good midfield player links the defensive and offensive phases with a combination of finding and creating space, dribbling, bringing his teammates into the play with a range of passes and creating scoring chances for the attackers. They will also be ready to shoot for goal or to run into areas ahead of the attackers when necessary.

It's obvious that central midfield players can cover a lot of ground during a match, and so need to have good stamina. They should also have good technical ability with the ball in controlling, dribbling, passing and shooting.

They also need to work on their awareness of what's happening in a game and of where opponents and teammates are, and to always be on the look-out for space and opportunities to pass the ball.

Whether you're an offensive midfielder, a defensive midfielder or a combination of both, you need to be an all-rounder with a full range of soccer abilities.

Central midfielders are often seen as the engine room of the team

WINGER

Everyone who has watched a game of soccer has thrilled to the skills of the winger, with his ability to beat defenders on the flanks with trickery and technique and deliver the ball to the strikers.

It's true that this is one of the most glamorous roles in the team, but don't be fooled into thinking that wingers don't have to put in their fair share of hard work. In most formations using wingers, they're asked to do a good bit of tracking back, closing down space and tackling to limit the opposition's chances of scoring.

When they're on the attack, however, wingers are great to watch, and a good winger can be a devastating weapon in a team's armoury. Using mostly the flank areas, but sometimes cutting infield to launch a shot on goal or link with the midfield and strikers, they pose a big threat.

If they choose to go outside their full back, beating them with pace or skill, then comes the opportunity to cross the ball into the danger areas.

What qualities and abilities do wingers need? As with full backs, it's often an advantage if a right winger is right-footed and a left winger is left-footed, but some right-footers have made more than competent left wingers.

Excellent ball control and dribbling, passing, crossing and shooting ability will be matched by a range of skills and techniques that will enable a winger to get past their markers, reach the goal line and pull the ball back for the strikers to launch an attack.

Speed, strength and tackling ability are other important assets, and bravery is needed to shrug off the tackles of defenders.

England's David Beckham is regarded as being one of the planet's greatest wingers

THE PERFECT POSITION?

There are variations on the positions featured in this chapter, for coaches often have different ideas on how soccer should be played and which team formations should be used. The ones we have talked about here are the most common positions in modern soccer, and it's plain to see there's a role for everyone, large or small. Which position do you see yourself filling?

The Brazilian star striker Ronaldo is feared by rival teams the world over

STRIKER

The central attacking players in professional soccer are so often the ones who get all the attention from the media and the headlines on the newspapers' back pages, but it's important to realize that not everyone can be a great striker. Some folks believe they're born, not made.

The strikers, usually taking up the most advanced positions in a team, are expected to take the goalscoring chances that come their way, either as a result of their own play or that of their teammates. They feed off the passes and crosses of colleagues to put opposing defenders and goalkeepers under pressure and keep the scoreboard ticking over.

Strikers may be asked to create space in the central areas by running out to the flanks, dragging central defenders with them, but most of the time they will occupy central positions. When the goalscoring opportunity arises, they are single-minded and determined to make the most of it. Some say that great strikers can even be described as selfish.

Another role of the striker is linking up the offensive play by providing a focus for passes from midfield players and defenders in the build-up. In fact, they're often called 'target men'.

Yet another role is the pressurizing of defenders as they try to start a phase of attacking play.

How would you spot a good potential striker? They tend to be well-built, perhaps taller than average (although some of the best strikers in the game have been below average height), with excellent shooting and heading techniques.

Ball control and strength are vital, and speed over a short distance is invaluable, as getting to the ball ahead of a defender is crucial. Stamina is important too: strikers can get through a lot of running during the course of a game.

It's a bonus if a striker can kick well with both feet, as there is often not enough time to shift the ball to one's preferred foot when a goalscoring chance comes along.

A good striker needs to be well-balanced and both mentally and physically tough .

TEAM TACTICS

Once you've worked out which playing position you're best at (and, just as importantly, which position you enjoy most), you have probably also discovered where you fit in best with your coach's favorite playing system.

There are many, many possible playing formations in soccer, and they've all been tried in competitive situations. But which is the most successful? The truth is that it's pretty much impossible to answer that question.

In order to find the best formation for his team, the coach has to bear a multitude of questions in mind. What are the strengths of his players? On the other hand, what are their weaknesses, and could one particular system cover them up? Which system are they most comfortable playing? Should he base his team's play on defense, or should he throw caution to the wind and go for all-out attack? What are his aims for a particular match, or for the season? Which systems are opposing teams likely to play? Which system has been good for him in the past?

Then there's the question of whether a coach should introduce a system at all. After all, soccer is above all meant to be fun, especially for youngsters, and there's a danger that, if things get too serious too soon, stars of the future will be put off the game for good.

And there's another danger: the coach who tries to teach his players too many systems, or who changes systems during matches when things start to go wrong, is running the risk of confusing the players. There's even a risk of the coach becoming confused – and that won't do the players or the team any good at all.

But we're assuming here that you've reached a level in your soccer where you're happy to think about systems and tactics, and your coach feels you're ready to do so.

The systems we're outlining in this chapter are only a few of the many formations soccer teams can play in – and the game's thinkers are forever coming up with new ideas.

But it's always best to start with the basics...

A packed stadium wants to see moments of brilliance out there on the field – but without the right formation, the crowd may leave bitterly disappointed

4 - 4 - 2

The 4-4-2 system has the advantage of being compact, it should be solid in midfield and it enables the midfield players to support both defenders and attackers quite easily.

One of its other major advantages is that it's often fairly simple to switch from 4-4-2 to a much more attacking 4-2-4, or even a 4-3-3, without too much disruption to the players or the need for many substitutions.

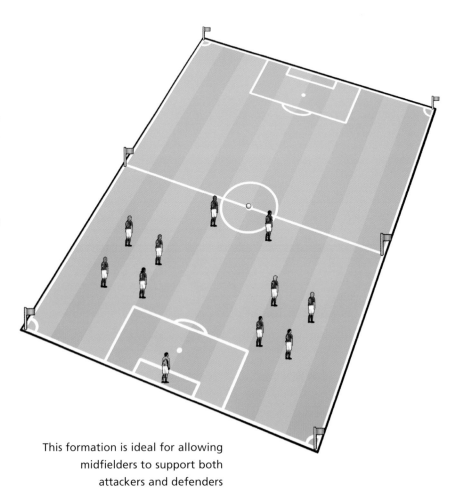

This formation is ideal for allowing
midfielders to support both
attackers and defenders

4 - 3 - 3

For the coach who wants to adopt a slightly more attacking system, the 4-3-3 is often ideal – especially late on in a game when goals may be much needed.

Using three attackers can have the effect of stretching the opponents' defense across the field and give the attack valuable width.

In the 4-3-3, the midfield players will often play closely together, while the two wide attackers can stay close to the touchlines (ready to drop back to share midfield duties if necessary), leaving a central striker to patrol the penalty area.

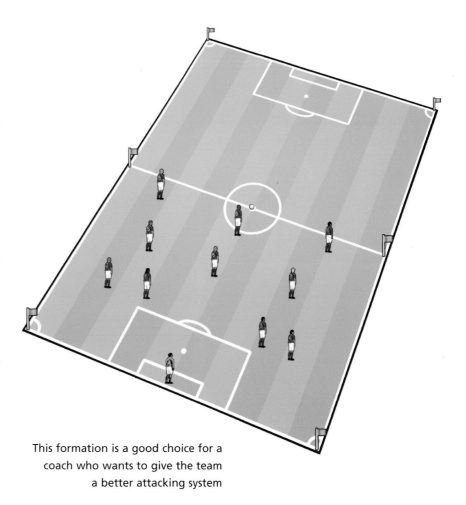

This formation is a good choice for a coach who wants to give the team a better attacking system

4 - 2 - 4

If your team's strengths lie in all-out attack, or if you need goals badly toward the end of a game, the 4-2-4 could be the ideal solution.

Needless to say, with four attacking players and just two midfielders, the '2' in the middle of the system are going to have to be fit and skilful, not only to distribute the ball effectively in offense but also to hold off the opponents' midfield when they have the ball.

But the 4-2-4, with its exciting attacking play through two wingers and two central strikers, can be great fun.

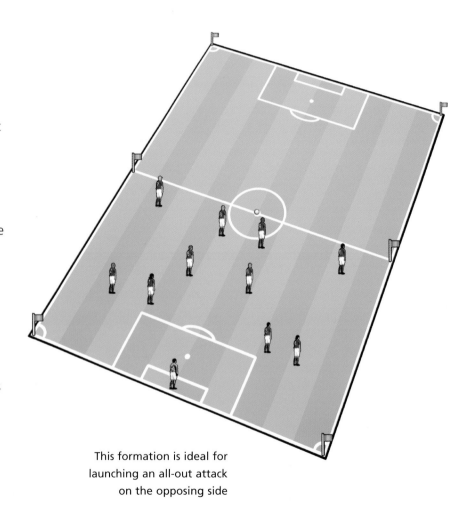

This formation is ideal for launching an all-out attack on the opposing side

4-5-1

In modern soccer, many teams opt to pack out the midfield – sometimes with as many as six players – to make it hard for opposing teams to find a way through toward the defense, and to make it easier to keep possession of the ball.

For the 4-5-1 to be effective, however, the lone striker must be able to keep running for the entire game, providing an outlet for passes forward, and to hold the ball up, waiting for his midfield teammates to support him.

This formation can be very effective in protecting a lead.

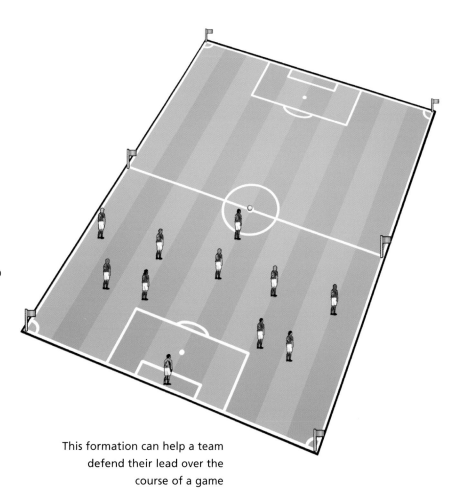

This formation can help a team defend their lead over the course of a game

4 - 4 - 1 - 1

The 4-4-1-1 formation can be seen as a variation of the 4-4-2, and it's similar in that it's compact in mid-field and defense and offers lots of attacking options.

The difference is that one of the attacking players tucks himself in between the midfield and his attacking teammate. This position, which aims to take advantage of space between the opponents' mid-field and defense, is sometimes called 'in the hole'.

This player, who should be skilful, with good ball control and passing, will be playing closely with the striker and should be ready to create and make the most out of scoring opportunities himself.

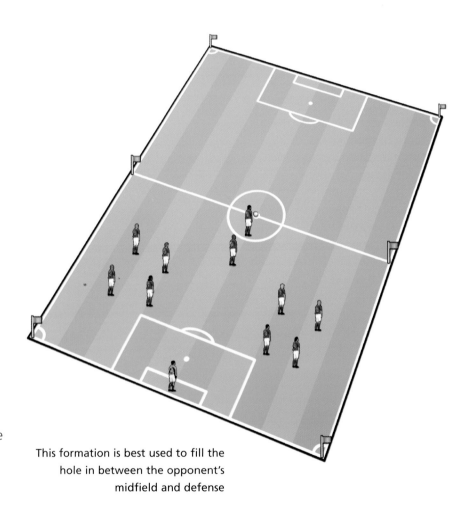

This formation is best used to fill the hole in between the opponent's midfield and defense

5-3-2

If your coach is looking for that bit of extra solidity in defense, he may well choose to adopt the useful 5-3-2 system.

In this formation, three central defenders play together as a unit – or sometimes with one dropping off to act as a sweeper – with two wide defenders picking up responsibility for the opposition's wingers.

These two defenders will often be asked to play as wing backs, which means they'll be in for a lot of running the length of the field, and they'll be equally comfortable attacking or defending.

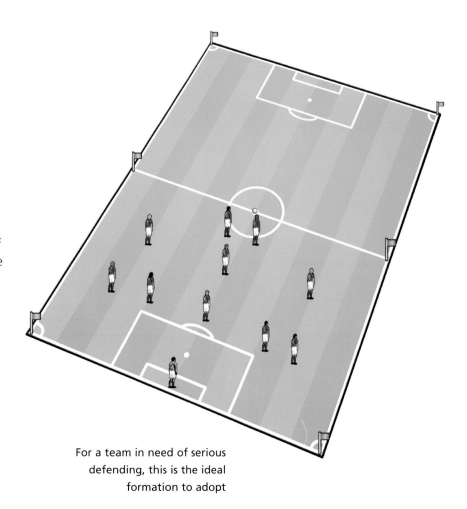

For a team in need of serious defending, this is the ideal formation to adopt

3 - 5 - 2

The 3-5-2 can be seen as a variation on the 5-3-2, and it's one of the most constantly popular systems in modern soccer.

Again, we have three defenders, who will benefit from the cover provided by a packed midfield. The wide midfield players will be expected to take on both defensive and offensive responsibilities as in the 5-3-2 system, and should be comfortable in both roles.

This system should be good for retaining possession of the ball and providing attacking chances for the two attackers, while the densely populated midfield should limit the opposing team's options.

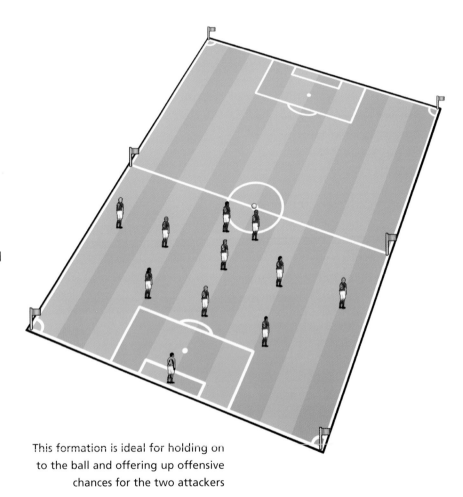

This formation is ideal for holding on to the ball and offering up offensive chances for the two attackers

3 - 4 - 3

Three defenders feature again in this formation, and they will often be covered by one of the midfield players, who will for much of the match be just in front of the defensive line. They are acting as a kind of sweeper and will aim to snuff out attacks before they reach the defense, and start off the team's attacking moves.

The 3-4-3 is an offensive formation, featuring three attackers, one of whom usually stays in the center of the field.

The wide attackers aim to occupy defenders in the flank areas.

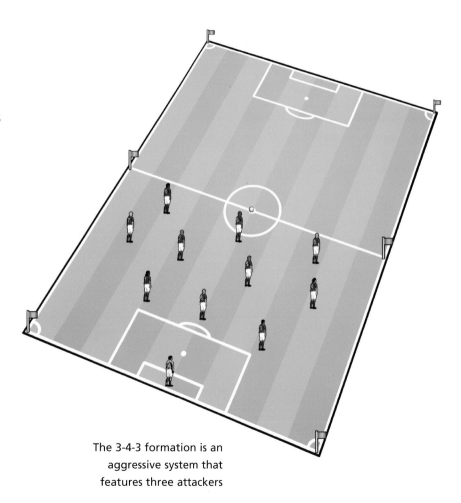

The 3-4-3 formation is an aggressive system that features three attackers

1 - 4 - 3 - 2

This formation – a variation of the 5-3-2 – can be successful if there's a player on your team who shows all the attributes of a good sweeper.

They will be the one who will be patrolling behind the defensive line of four, looking out for any real threats that have been missed by the team's defenders.

Don't forget that the sweeper will sometimes be free to step forward to boost the midfield, and even the attack on some occasions.

This formation should be very compact, with two hard-working attackers who should be able to benefit from the creative work going on behind them.

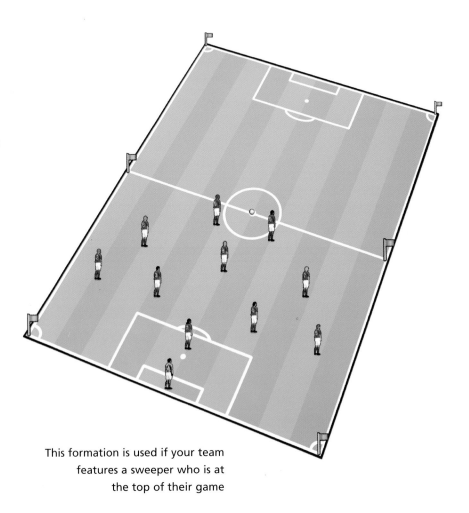

This formation is used if your team features a sweeper who is at the top of their game

1 - 3 - 4 - 2

This is another soccer formation that uses the services of a sweeper, but this time they will be playing behind a defensive line of three.

Once again, the sweeper will often be able to initiate attacks as well as provide the last line of defense before the goalkeeper, so they should be versatile, skilful players.

A compact defense and midfield give this system a solid look, and again the forward players must be prepared to get through a lot of work, roaming to all parts of the final third of the field.

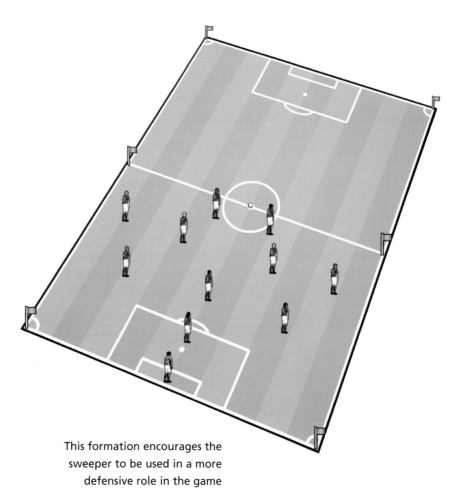

This formation encourages the sweeper to be used in a more defensive role in the game

TECHNICAL MATTERS

Pictured here is the soccer legend Diego Maradona who helped Argentina win the World Cup in 1986

Next time you're watching a soccer match in a stadium or on TV, stop and marvel at just how many techniques and skills the top players have mastered in their careers.

They are able to control the ball with one touch, regardless of whether it's with their knees, feet or chests. They can also keep the ball under close control at their feet as they run along, while looking around to see what teammates and rival players are doing.

These professional players are also masters of passing, and they can do it with every available part of their foot, be it inside, outside or instep.

When it comes to crossing the ball into the danger area, or shooting for goal from a short or a long distance, the top players have all the necessary techniques and skills at their disposal – and the very best can perform them with either foot.

The top players also have complete control over the ball when it comes to heading. They know when a little flick of the ball with the head is all that's needed, or when a powerful header will send the ball away from danger – or hurtling straight into

the back of the net! They know how to kick a stationary ball to make it swerve in the air, and how to send it soaring in a perfectly straight trajectory.

All a team's players, and not just the defenders, know the best ways to tackle an opponent, too. They also understand when it's best not to commit themselves to a tackle but to contain their opponent in the space they are occupying.

They also know how to slide tackle, how to block tackle, and how to hook the ball away from behind in the blink of an eye.

Even those players adored by their fans need to keep practicing their skills to stay at the top of their game

The best players are able to create space on the field for themselves and their teammates, and they know how to make the very most of that space.

The top goalkeepers have practiced all the skills needed to protect the goal many times over – from parrying, diving and deflecting through to catching, punching and throwing, their skills seem endless!

Nor should you forget that pro players can display all these tough techniques at high speed when under pressure from opponents.

Soccer is a very fast game and it sometimes seems as if professional players are performing all these techniques without even thinking about them, such is their speed, skill and confidence.

Maybe at this point you're thinking: 'I'll never be able to do all that.' But you should always remember that the techniques that the pro players show off on the pitch with such ease didn't come to them like a bolt from the blue!

They had to master their skills, just like you, and they had to practice them over and over again to truly perfect them.

And even the best-paid, most glamorous stars in soccer go back to the basics all the time when they are off the pitch. It's vital for any player to rehearse and reinforce those fundamental skills continually. In soccer, as in so many other areas of life, you never stop learning.

So don't despair if you're thinking you'll never master all the skills. The secret is enthusiasm, dedication and long hours of practice. After all, you wouldn't expect to become a concert pianist overnight now, would you?

In this chapter, we'll be introducing you to these basic techniques of soccer so you can begin honing your skills. So now it's over to you, your coach – and some serious practice.

CONTROL

Controlling the ball is the most basic of all soccer techniques. If you don't have good ball control once it's been passed to you, you won't be able to do anything with it!

It's also one of the most difficult techniques to master. Even at high levels in the game, you will some-times see highly-paid professionals failing to control the ball properly, with the result that his or her team is put under huge pressure as the opposition gains possession.

So you should work hard on your control, with your coach encouraging you and pointing out where you're going wrong. And it's important to remember that you will get it wrong at first, possibly many times – but don't worry because everybody does.

Let's assume that a teammate has passed the ball to you along the ground. What should you do in order to bring it under control with one of your feet?

- Make sure you are in line with the ball's path. If that means moving into position with some quick footwork, do it.
- Decide which foot you are going to use to control the ball, and which part of the foot. Again, you may need some footwork here to adjust your position. It's ideal to be able to control the ball with the side of your foot.
- Watch the ball carefully. It's important not to be tense, so relax your body and keep your head steady as you go.
- As the ball arrives, your foot should 'give' with the ball, cushioning the impact. This means you'll be pulling your foot back slightly in the direction the ball is moving.
- Once you have the ball under control, you can start to think about the options open to you – such as passing, dribbling or shooting.

But what if the ball arrives in the air, and not along the ground? Here you have two main options for controlling the ball: your thigh and your chest.

- If you're using a thigh, the technique is not very different from using a foot.
- Position yourself in the path of the ball. Don't forget your footwork, and watch the ball! Lift one foot so that a thigh is in the correct position.
- Cushion the ball as it touches your thigh by 'giving' and dropping your foot to the ground.
- Controlling the ball with your chest is a different matter, and it's a difficult technique to truly master. Position yourself so that you are front-on to the path of the ball.
- Puff out your chest as the ball comes closer.
- As the ball touches your chest, pull back to deaden the impact.

And practice, practice, practice!

PASSING

Good passing is the basic building block of soccer success. Sure, it's exciting to set off on a daring dribble with the ball at your feet, beating defender after defender – and it's even more exciting to then smash the ball high into the roof of the net!

But, without passing, there is no basis for those thrilling moves, and every player in the world has practiced his or her passing techniques endlessly. And, for those in the know, there's just as much enjoyment to be had from watching a well-constructed passing manoeuvre flowing from one end of the field to the other.

The sidefoot pass can be practiced at almost any time – you don't even need any other players! Try kicking a ball against a wall with your new technique (making sure it doesn't annoy your neighbors). Pass against the wall, control with one touch, then pass again – and don't forget to use both feet.

Also, remember that the best players can pass with either foot, so while you're practicing your passing, make sure you use both feet equally. It may not feel natural at first to use your 'wrong' foot, but, if you keep it up, you will become a true 'two-footed' player one day.

Let's start with the sidefoot pass...
- Why is the sidefoot pass usually the most accurate of passes? Because you are striking the ball with a large area of your foot, and also because it's the easiest soccer passing technique to learn.
- Adjust your feet to ensure they are in the right position, and the ball is within a comfortable distance. Your non-kicking foot should be alongside the ball and pointing toward your intended target.
- Watch the ball and keep your head steady. Your head should be directly over the ball so that your body weight is too. If you lean back, the ball will probably leave the ground when you pass it.
- You should be well balanced, so use your arms to steady yourself ready for the pass.
- With a short backlift of your kicking leg, and with your ankle and knee locked, 'push' through the ball to send it on its way. Don't forget to follow through with your foot, so that it is facing your target all the time.

● When you and your coach are happy with your sidefoot technique, it may be time to move on to longer passes, when the ball is played in the air. Here, it's useful to think of the pass being made with your shoelaces.

● Your non-kicking foot should be positioned to one side of the ball and slightly behind it, so that your body weight is behind it too. Remember – head steady! Be balanced! And watch the ball!

● Kick through the bottom half of the ball, with the shoelaces part of your foot, so that it leaves the ground.

● Don't forget to follow through.

● You will need a large area, as well as a partner, to practice this passing technique properly.

● Soon, you can start thinking about widening your repertoire by using the inside and outside of your foot. But, for now, just focus on the basics!

SHOOTING

Picture the scene – a shot from outside the penalty area whistles past the goalie into the net. The spectators, attackers and coaches go crazy while the defending team looks on in disbelief and horror.

Football is all about scoring and stopping goals, and a good shooting technique is therefore invaluable. Whether it's a rocket of a shot hit on the half-volley from a corner kick or a simple sidefoot tap-in from a few meters out, they all count.

But here's the thing to remember about shooting: it's simply 'passing' the ball into the goal, no more and no less, and those passing techniques you've been busy practicing are the ones you will use when the opportunity to shoot comes along.

Shooting the soccer ball into the back of the net is every soccer player's dream – but mastering the art takes years of dedication. Pictured here is AC Milan's Andriy Shevchenko showing why his shooting skills are regarded as among the best in the world

Balance, concentration, control and accuracy are vital, so here are a few tips to get you on the right path to becoming a shooting star.

● Before you shoot, you should be as aware as you can be of where the goalie and defenders are positioned, and which area of the goal is most vulnerable. Often, shooting opportunities happen so fast that there's little time to look around, but do your best.

● Be sure in your own mind which technique you are going to use for your shot. You probably already know which foot you're going to use, but would it best to side-foot the ball for maximum accuracy? Or is power more important, and would a blast from the instep/shoelaces area of your boot do the trick? Perhaps you've been working on curving the ball in the air and you'd like to try it out on the field. Or maybe a chip over the goalie would be best.

● Whichever technique you decide on, your shot has to be accurate. A shot that misses a post by a hair's breadth does no more damage than one that lands near the corner flag – the old saying 'a miss is as good as a mile' is very appropriate here. So concentrate on hitting the target and making the goalkeeper really work hard.

● Be balanced, be steady and make sure your body weight is over the ball. These are things we've already learned in the section about passing, and they're just as important in shooting. Sure, it's not always actually possible to be perfectly balanced when shooting or passing, but bear in mind that the more prepared you are to kick the ball, the better your shot will be. Remember to follow through with your kicking leg every time.

● Our old friend the wall is a reliable practice partner when it comes to shooting, if you can't wait to gather some friends for a session. Check you're not causing a nuisance, then shoot against the wall, control the ball and then shoot again, making sure you're using both feet equally.

DRIBBLING

Dribbling with the ball is a great soccer technique, but it's also one of the hardest to learn. You need speed, agility, bravery and above all great ball control. Some folks say great dribblers are born, not made, but there's no doubting that anyone can learn some of the tricks of the trade.

Before learning how to dribble the ball past opponents, you should first learn when to perform this delicate technique – and when to leave it well alone. It's a good rule of thumb to remember that dribbling should be confined to the attacking half of the field – after all, your defenders are unlikely to applaud you if you embark on a run on the edge your own penalty area. It's far too risky.

We've all been thrilled at the sight of a skilful winger dribbling his way along the touch line, leaving a trail of defenders in his wake as he twists, turns, feints and surges on and on…

Here are some top tips for good dribbling:

● Keep control of the ball at all times. The ball should never be too far away from your feet, and you shouldn't be running faster than the ball is traveling.

● Keep your head up while you're running. You need to keep yourself aware of what's happening around you. Is that big defender going to come in with a slide tackle? Is that team-mate making a good run into a space where a pass will give him or her a scoring chance? Is now the right time to cross the ball into the penalty area?

● Work on your ability to change the pace at which you're running. Nothing is more effective at beating a defender than pushing the ball past him or her and then, with a surge of pace, running past to pick up the ball again.

● Work on your ability to change the direction you're running in, too. A sudden change of direction in your dribble, with the ball still at your feet, can sometimes 'wrong-foot' an entire defense!

● Practice your ability to wrong-foot a defender by another means – perhaps pretending to go in one direction by dropping one shoulder before sprinting off in the other

with the ball still at your feet. There is nothing like a real, live game situation for showing off your dribbling techniques, and a lot can be accomplished during coaching sessions, but if you're determined to put in some extra practice on your own, go ahead.

To practice dribbling, you'll need a large area. If you haven't any cones, lay a series of other objects on the ground. Then off you go, weaving backward and forward between them with the ball seemingly tied to your feet!

CROSSING

The cross from one of the flank areas into the middle of the field, with attackers running on to it, is one of the most devastating passes you can make – especially if it's made from near the goal line and lands behind the defense.

Some pro soccer players have made very good careers out of being expert ball crossers and they're worth their weight in gold. But these players are also known for their ability to make the right decision when it comes to crossing the ball.

And making the right decision depends on your awareness of what's happening. Where are the goalkeeper, defenders and attackers positioned? Which type of cross would be most dangerous to the

While everyone wants to be the player who kicks the ball into the goal, a skilled team member who knows how to make the perfect cross is vital to any game's success – and one of the best crossers in the world is Brazil's Roberto Carlos

defense? Should it be driven or curled in?

Maybe you should cross the ball to the back post, but not too close or else the goalie could pluck it out of the air. Maybe an attacker is

making a run to the near post, where he could profit from a well-delivered early cross. Perhaps a cut-back toward the back of the penalty area, where midfielders are making threatening runs, is called for.

Crossing the ball is simply another way of passing it, and you will be using the same basic techniques. However, there's another option that's a valuable crossing technique and we'll take a look at it here – swerving the ball through the air using the inside of your foot.

● Your non-kicking foot should be to the side of the ball and slightly behind it. Remember – balance! Head steady! Body weight over the ball! And watch the ball!

● Kick the outside of the ball with the inside of your foot. Follow through with your leg moving across and away from your body.

The ball should now be curving through the air and away from the goalkeeper, wrong-footing defenders and inviting your teammates to attack it with head or foot. You too can learn to bend it like Beckham!

● Learning to swerve the ball through the air means many hours of practice with both a stationary and a moving ball, and it can be done during coaching sessions. But for the really dedicated player, solitary practice is by no means out of the question, although it may mean lots of running from one side of your practice area to the other to gather the ball. Make sure you have plenty of space, and don't forget to practice with both feet.

HEADING

Of all the techniques used in soccer, heading the ball is often the last one to be taught because it's of far greater importance in the adult game than among youngsters. Very young players tend not to lift the ball far off the ground anyway, so the opportunity for a header doesn't arise too often.

Then there's the fact that some young players are a little fearful of heading the ball. They're often the ones you see closing their eyes and letting the ball bounce off the tops of their heads, without controlling where it goes.

When teaching heading, many coaches working with young players start them off with a soft ball before progressing to a proper soccer ball. Whatever ball you're using though, the technique remains the same:

● Keep your eyes on the ball as it approaches you.

● Position yourself in line with the ball. Footwork might be needed here so always try to remain aware of the positioning of your feet.

● Remember to balance and always concentrate on what you are doing. Using your forehead, head the center of the ball, driving your head forward just as it makes contact with the ball.

● And practice, practice, practice! Your coach will be keen to set up some heading drills as you progress in the game, but as ever there are options for the solitary player. Practice bouncing the ball against a wall and heading it back and, as you progress, see how many times you can head it without letting it hit the ground. You'll find you'll be using all kinds of heading variations as the ball changes direction, and it's great for practicing getting into the correct position.

However, watch an adult player practice his heading and you'll see why the technique is so important if you want to progress in the game. A talented player will watch the ball all the way, then make firm contact with it using his forehead before sending the ball exactly where he wants it to go.

Heading is a very important technique for defenders, attackers and midfield players struggling to win possession. Plus a powerfully headed clearance will bring as much satisfaction to a player as a skilful header into the top corner of the net.

Manchester United's Rio Ferdinand is a master of the tackle

TACKLING

Don't run away with the idea that tackling is just for defenders. Every player on the team should have tackling in his armory of skills – it's worth bearing in mind that when your opponents have possession of the ball, every player on your team becomes in reality a defender. You need that ball back – and you need it back fast!

So take your tackling sessions seriously, no matter which position you play in. Even goalkeepers can get involved, as there's no telling when a no-hands, last-ditch tackle by your goalie might be needed to save the day.

There are many, many ways of tackling to take the ball away from an opponent, but here we're going to look at some of the basics. What, then, are the fundamentals of good tackling?

● Make sure you are within easy reach of the ball before committing yourself to a tackle. There are several reasons for this: you will be able to get your full weight behind the tackle; you will reduce the chances of you or your opponent being injured; and your opponent will find it less easy to avoid the tackle.

● Be patient. There's a right time and a wrong time to commit yourself. You will learn more about this as you pick up experience in the game, but for now, the right time is when you are close enough and in the right position to be confident about winning your challenge for the ball.

● In a front-on, block-type tackle, try to make contact with the center of the ball. Too high on the ball and you risk losing the tackle and injuring your opponent; too low and the ball may bounce up out of control. And your knee and ankle should be 'locked' in place, otherwise it may be you who ends up injured.

● Make sure you are fully committed when you go into the tackle. Use as much strength and weight as you can. Be bold.

There really is no good way of practicing tackling other than in a coaching session – a wall is clearly no good here! In the meantime, your coach will help you to learn other tackling techniques as you gain more and more experience.

GOALKEEPING

It's one of the most gripping sights in sports: the goalkeeper seemingly flying through the air to pluck the ball away from danger. But there's so much more to the goalkeeper's game than this rather glamorous kind of save.

Sure, you're the only player on the field who's allowed to handle the ball, but you need to earn that right by mastering the techniques of catching, punching, diving, parrying, deflecting, kicking, throwing – yes, the list is endless and never has a specialist been asked to perform quite so many tasks. If you're looking for an easy life on the pitch, then the position of goalkeeper is most certainly not for you!

There are certain basics to the goalkeeper's art that must be practiced again and again before they can progress to more advanced techniques. And none is more basic than catching the ball. Your coach will be eager to drum the following points into you as he teaches you how the best goalies in the business catch the ball:

● Your feet should be shoulder-width apart as you prepare to catch the ball.
● Your weight should be on the balls (the front parts) of your feet. That will give you a good starting point if you need to move to make the catch.

● Your hands should be at the same height as your waist, with the palms of your gloves open. Your hands should also be outside the line of your body for a wider surface area.
● Keep your eyes on the ball and stay focused and balanced.
● Watch the ball all the way into your hands.
● Pull the ball in tight to your body.

There are variations on the basic catch, of course. For example, what happens when the ball is above head height? Here's what you should do:
● Have your hands in front of your body as the ball approaches.
● Spread your fingers to make a 'W'

shape, with your thumbs nearly touching each other.
● Catch behind the ball.
● Gather it to your body.

For a catch at chest height, you could go for either of the techniques just described, finishing off the technique by clasping the ball to your chest.

Regular coaching drills will help you to perfect your catching technique. And out of hours, a simple wall will prove invaluable. Bouncing a ball against one should give you all the practice you need until it's time for your next match.

SUMMARY

You'll have noticed reading this chapter that there are some things that are required in all soccer techniques: keeping a steady eye on the ball, getting your position right and being aware of the play going on around you.

Whatever technique you're rehearsing, if you keep those basics in mind, you will be a pleasure to coach – and you'll enjoy your soccer more.

PRACTICE MAKES PERFECT

Now is when the fun starts. This is the time you get to run out on the field of play and kick a soccer ball around to your heart's content. This chapter is all about putting your techniques into practice, and then improving them, in a practice session.

Your coach, without doubt, has plenty of ideas to help you enjoy your soccer while at the same time molding you and your friends into a great team, but here we're only looking at fun ways to improve your game.

Some of the following drills, which are all in the form of games, can even be practiced outside regular coaching sessions, as they can be adapted so that they use very little equipment. If there's just you and a couple of friends kicking a ball around in the park, try one of these games to bring a little variety into the session.

So the message is: enjoy your coaching sessions as much as you enjoy your full games. There are many laughs to be had while you strengthen your skills. But there are a few words of warning, too, for young players and coaches. Don't overdo it. As we'll see in the next chapter, doing too much physical work at too young an age can be dangerous.

Always dress correctly (the sun can be cruel), and make sure you have enough water to last a session. Read the next chapter for details. And here's a little warning for youngsters starting out in soccer and for the coaches looking after them: please don't concentrate too much on repeated heading of the ball. Studies have shown that soccer balls can have a nasty effect on young heads, and on the brains inside them, if too much heading is asked of them. So, that's the serious stuff over. Now let's get on with the fun!

THE WALL

This game is good for players working on their ball-receiving technique. You need one ball and you can have as many players as you want. All players line up in teams, in single file. One player (the wall) leaves his or her team and faces the line, about 16.4ft/5m or more away.

The player at the head of the line then passes the ball to the wall, who controls it, leaves the ball and runs to the back of the line. The next player runs to become the wall and passes back to the next player in line, who in turn passes to the new wall.

When every player has had a turn at being the wall, the line sits down. The first team to be sitting is declared the winner.

BODY PARTS

This is another game that teaches ball control, but it encourages you to use feet, chest and thighs. One ball is needed. Players line up in single file facing the coach. As each player gets to about 16.4ft/5m of the coach, the coach will call 'left foot', 'right foot', 'left thigh', 'right thigh' or 'chest'. He then throws the ball to the player, who has to control it with the part of the body called. The player passes the ball back to the coach and runs to the back of the line, and the next player takes their place.

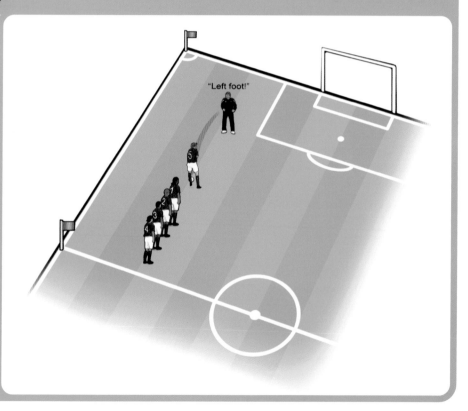

"Left foot!"

THROUGH THE CONES

For this passing game you need four players and 12 cones, laid out in a 49ft/15m-square grid, as shown in the illustration. You'll also need two balls. The players, in two teams of two, are placed on each of the four sides of the grid, with teammates facing each other.

The aim of the game is for each player to pass his or her ball to a teammate between the eight cones facing him or her. First team to five wins! This game is really good for improving the accuracy of your passing, so you should focus on making your passes more accurate rather than powerful.

SHOOT!

You can use a penalty area for this game, or have your coach mark out an area of the same size with cones. You also need two cones about 16.4ft/5m apart, placed near the edge of the penalty area. Other essential equipment: plenty of balls. One player is the goalkeeper and another is the striker. The other players line up just outside the penalty area.

The striker makes a run around the two cones and receives a pass from the player at the head of the line. He or she controls the ball and tries to shoot past the keeper, who tries to save. The striker can then become the keeper or, if you want to give your regular keeper more practice, run to the back of the line.

GIVE AND GO

This is a very simple game that should help build your passing and controlling techniques. Two lines of players, in single file, face each other. The player at the head of one line passes the ball to the player at the head of the other line and runs on to receive the one-two pass, which should be played to the side or behind.

The runner returns the ball to the player who passed the ball to them and joins the back of the line. The game goes on until all players have played each role in the 'give and go'.

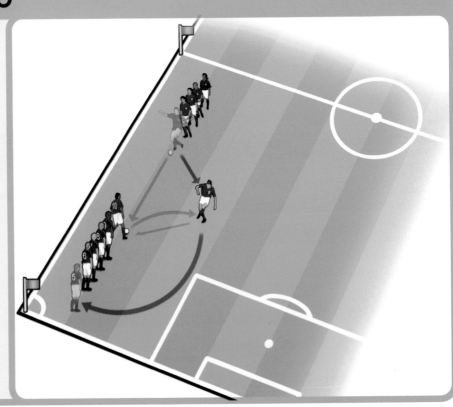

NAME OF THE GAME

You only need one ball for this passing and control-ling game, but you need a good few players, who are arranged in a circle. The game is quite simple: players, before they pass the ball to a teammate – who can be anywhere in the circle – have to call out the receiver's name.

If the ball ends up at any player other than the one who's been named, the passer has to take the ball back and make a new pass – calling out loudly the new target's name, of course.

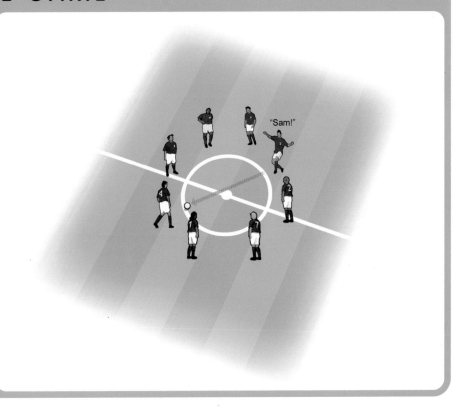

CRISS-CROSS

This is another simple game that gives players practice in crossing the ball and goalkeepers practice in collecting it in the air or on the ground. Use a penalty area or similar area marked out with cones. The players line up outside the penalty area and the lead player runs out toward the touch line and on to a pass delivered by the coach toward the goal line.

The player takes one touch to control the ball and crosses the ball into the center, where the goalie will collect it and pass it back to the coach.

KEEPY-UPPY

This game is excellent practice for your ball control skills, plus it's very, very simple.

You can play with as few as two players, but if you have more they should be in a circle. The rules are easy: keep the ball in the air, without letting it touch the ground, as the ball is passed between players.

You can take as many touches as you want to control the ball and pass it on, and you can use any part of the body except your hands.

USE YOUR HEAD

This game encourages you to use the heading techniques you've been learning without asking players to head the ball again and again. Two teams of four players play with one ball in a 98ft/30m x 49ft/15m area, with small goals at either end.

It's a normal practice game, except that goals scored from a header count as two points, rather than the usual one. Your coach might even want to award a point every time a player heads the ball.

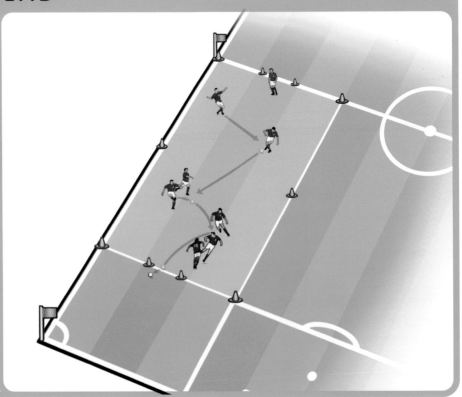

UP AND DOWN

Here's another game played in a 98ft/30m x 49ft/15m area, with small goals marked out at each end. Two teams of four or more players each try to move from one end of the area to the other, and score a goal. How? One player throws the ball to a teammate, who heads it on to another teammate, who then catches it.

This player then throws the ball to another teammate, who heads it, and so on, as the team moves toward its goal. But the ball passes to the opposing team if the ball is dropped or otherwise touches the ground.

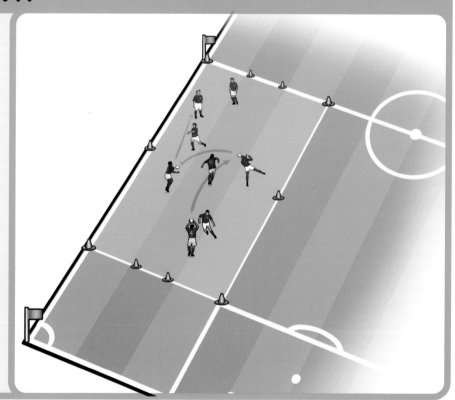

DON'T MAKE A SOUND

This simple game encourages goalies to use 'soft hands' to receive the ball, so that it doesn't bounce off their gloves. One player serves the ball to the goalkeeper by throwing it to them – the service can be hard or soft, high or low.

A point is awarded every time the keeper makes a catch without a sound coming from his gloves. Be warned, though: it's much, much harder than it sounds.

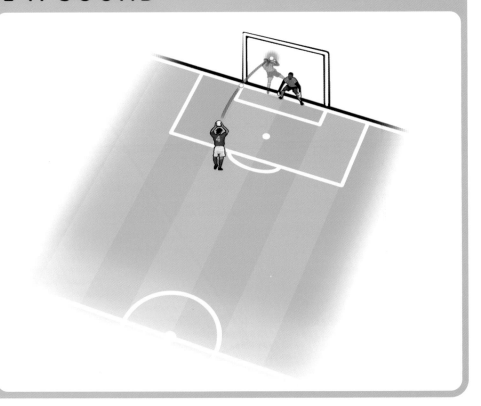

ONE AT A TIME

Your coach will mark out quite a large area for this team practice game, which should use just about every soccer technique. Two teams try to score in fairly small goals defended by goalies – nothing too unusual there. But they have to do so with every single player on the team touching the ball at least once.

The more players there are in each team, the harder it will be to bring everybody into the play – and the more fun it will be. You could even use a rule forbidding running with the ball, for more fun.

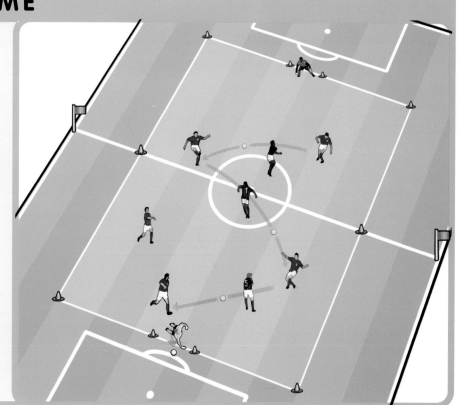

PRESSURE PLAY

You will need one ball for each group of three players for this excellent game. Player A (defender) passes the ball to player B and runs immediately to pressure the receiver, who is aiming to control the ball and pass it to player C. Player A, of course, tries to win the ball. If player B completes their pass, they then pick up the ball and become player A. If player A wins the ball, they then get to deliver the ball to player B again.

BOTH SIDES

This is a very simple two-versus-two game, but it has a twist – goals can be scored from either side of a single goal marked out with cones. One team starts with the ball and aims to score through a combination of passing, moving and dribbling, while the other team attempts to defend and prevent a goal – tricky when the goal actually has two sides!

If team A succeeds in scoring, possession of the ball switches to team B. This game should be played for a short time – three minutes at most, as there's a lot of chasing, tackling and pressurizing to do. It's ideal for keeping you fit!

ZONES AND CONES

For this passing and dribbling game, your coach should lay out a grid, 66ft/20m x 132ft/40m, with eight cones, as illustrated. Six or eight players are needed, in two teams.

One team is defending its zone while the other attacks it, trying to pass and dribble its way into the opposite zone. If it succeeds, it scores a point and the ball passes to the other team, which must try to score a point itself. Try this game for five or ten minutes – tiring but huge fun!

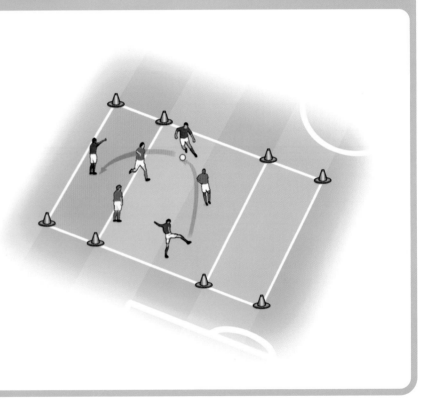

TWO BY TWO

For this game, good for passing, dribbling and defending, you need a 49ft/15m x 66ft/20m grid marked out, with small goals at each end. Teams of two players start by competing for a ball thrown in by the coach and the successful team aims to score a goal through dribbling and passing around its opponents. The other team then tries to stop it by tackling or intercepting.

If the ball goes out of play, it's rolled in again by a member of the team that put it out of play.

The first team to a certain number of goals wins – and you'll probably find that three goals is enough!

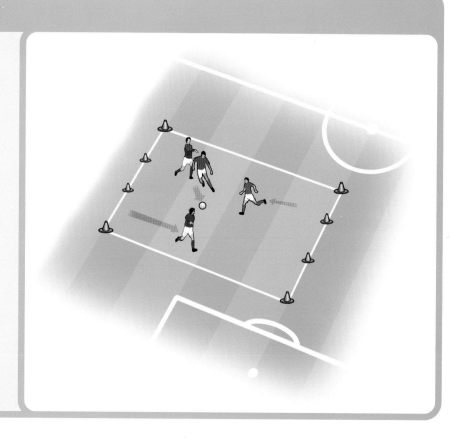

FIT FOR THE JOB

Are you fit for soccer? Although most youngsters are naturally fit and perfectly capable of playing a full part in most sports, there are ways of making sure you can perform just that little bit better.

Ask yourself: why am I playing soccer? The chances are that your answer is: "Because I love it!" Soccer is fun. The world's greatest sport is also a great way of keeping fit, learning new skills and making new friends.

And, of course, there's nothing like the feeling you get when you score a winning goal or lift a trophy at the end of a long, hard season. But there is a way of ensuring that you enjoy your soccer even more than you do right now.

All you have to do is take a few extra steps toward a higher level of fitness, healthy eating and drinking, and a sensible attitude to the game. A fit, healthy you will enjoy your soccer even more – and that's a promise.

In this chapter, we're going to look at ways of ensuring that you're properly prepared for playing soccer, in both body and mind. We'll talk about fitness and the absolute importance of warming up properly before exercise, and of cooling down afterward.

We'll look at why it's so important to follow a balanced, healthy diet and find out what's best to eat and drink before, during and also after a game.

We'll also take a look at the inner you and discover that a healthy attitude to soccer is important. And, finally, we'll provide some tips on how to deal with soccer injuries.

PHYSICAL FITNESS

If you love soccer, it's a pretty good bet that you love other sports and that your life is fairly active. You probably prefer getting out in the open air and running just for the fun of it to staying in your room, playing video games or watching your television.

In other words, you're probably pretty physically fit already – fit enough to enjoy your soccer and fit enough to play a full game. Young players shouldn't really need to follow a special fitness program, and your coach will explain to you the dangers of training too much at an age when your body is growing fast. When you're older – say in your early- to mid-teens – you might want to start thinking about a soccer conditioning program.

But, for now, playing soccer regularly, combined with a coaching program, will keep you fit, and you could certainly add activities like swimming, cycling, running or

Activities like cycling can help you keep fit – and also give you some time away from the pitch to recharge

basketball to your regular rota, if you don't practice them already. They're all really good for your heart and respiratory system.

The secret is not to do too much, and to make sure you're eating and drinking healthily. If you find you're getting overtired from your exercise, you're probably overdoing it and you should talk to your parents or your coach about it.

On the other hand, there's a vital part of soccer conditioning that should start off every coaching session and game – the warm-up. Why is warming up so important? Well, there are actually several reasons to consider.

Warming up your muscles will get the most out of them, because a warm muscle works much better than a cold one. Warming up by stretching your muscles also

If you have any questions or worries about your fitness, then talk to your coach or your parents. That's what they are there for!

makes you less likely to suffer an injury during play, as it makes you more flexible.

If your coach doesn't get you warmed up properly for training sessions or matches, you should point this out to them.

The important thing to remember about warming up is to take it slowly, building up the speed very gradually. For young kids, it can start off with a simple exercise like very light jogging on the spot, perhaps tapping the top of a football with your left foot, then your right foot as you jog up and down.

Stretching gently is great for warming up

A simple dribbling session can also help you to get warmed up: your coach should set up an area in which you and your teammates can run slowly with balls at your feet, helping you to get your hearts pumping and warming your muscles. Again, remember to start slowly and gradually increase speed.

Stretching your leg and back muscles lightly will also help, and your coach can show you how to do this properly. It's important to stretch, though, not to bounce.

So you're ready to play the game, and you'll enjoy it even more because you're properly warmed up.

Practice with your teammates or simply by yourself to loosen your body up ready for soccer

But guess what? You're not through yet. Just as important as the warm-up is the vital cool-down period.

Why? Light exercise after heavy exercise helps your body to get rid of the nasty stuff that's built up in your system as your muscles have worked hard; it helps to stop your muscles getting stiff and sore; and it helps your heart to pump the blood round your body efficiently.

So it's back to a little light jogging and stretching for a few minutes after the practice or game. You can pretty much follow the same pattern of exercises you used for the warm-up, but remember to take it slowly and gently. You don't want to get injured now, of all times!

FOOD

Come on, you know it already! Eating healthily is the right thing to do, and helps you in every area of your life. No one's saying the occasional burger with fries or a chewy candy bar from time to time will ruin your life for ever. They won't, obviously.

But it's important to have a proper balance in your diet – and if you have an active lifestyle, playing soccer whenever you can, it's extra important to feed your body in the correct way.

Your body, just like a car, needs fuel if it's going to work efficiently. And, just like a car, it needs the correct fuel. So which kinds of food and drink are going to help you enjoy your soccer, and help you perform that little bit better? Let's start by taking a look at

Burgers are tasty – and that's a fact. But too many are not going to do your fitness any good at all…

food. Despite what adults tell you about the dangers of eating too much sugar (and they're right), it's actually a sugar that enables your muscles to do all the work that's needed in a game of soccer. But don't rush out and stock up on candy: the sugar you need is a certain kind, and it's called glucose. Your body takes glucose and changes it into a substance

Don't even think about it…

called glycogen, and then it's ready to act as a fuel for your muscles.

The best way to make sure you're getting enough glucose into your body is by following a balanced diet, with plenty of food like bread, potatoes, pasta, cereals and fresh fruit and vegetables. And that's especially important before a

Oranges are sweet, tasty
and very good for you
and your body

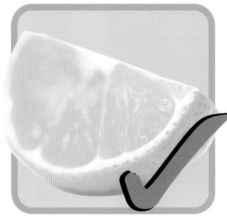

Ask your family to get in
healthy food to help
your performance

vegetables, with maybe some
chicken or fish. And, if you feel the
need for a snack before the game,
why not try an energy bar, some
more fruit or some yogurt?

The same goes for during the
game itself. If you need a snack at
half-time, go for something simple
like fruit – oranges were popular
for many years, although nowa-
days they say mango is great. And
don't despair if you think you'll
never see a candy bar again – they
can be good for an occasional
treat after a game.

And after the game is when you
should be looking to replace the
fuel your body has used up on the
field. Your coach or parents should
make sure you have a good,
healthy meal as soon as possible
after play has finished.

game. But when is the best time
to actually eat?

A good rule for youngsters is that
they should eat little and often.
Snacking needn't be a bad thing if
the snacks are healthy. But for a
main, pre-match meal, you should
be looking at eating two or three
hours beforehand, giving your
body a good chance of digesting

properly before you ask it to do
any exercise.

Let's look at what you should be
eating in that pre-match meal.
Please forget about that burger
and fries, and do try and ignore
that candy bar!

Your meal should include good
stuff like pasta, cereals, fruit and

DRINK

Your body loses a lot of water during exercise, and it can't work properly if it's low on water. So you need to keep the fluid level in your body properly topped up all the time before, during and after exercise, using our motto of 'little and often'. And that means even if you're not really thirsty.

You should drink plenty of water with your pre-match meal, and keep it going as you go through the warm-up – regular little sips of water will help your body perform better. Whenever you can during the game, take some more water on board, and afterward you will need to put back into your body the water you've lost during play. Of course, all these tips about drinking plenty are especially important in hot weather, which can be really tough on players of all ages.

Water might not be as enticing as cola but you'll need plenty of it to keep your body hydrated

Should you always drink water rather than one of the fancy sports drinks you see on the supermarket shelves? A good answer is: 'Water is best, but a little sports drink now and again won't harm you.' But you don't have to rely on expensive sports drinks. Afer all, fruit juice mixed with water makes a tasty alternative and will be much cheaper.

What you shouldn't be drinking before and during a game are fizzy sodas and colas.

It's always great when the sun comes out but it can drain your body of vital fluids

Can't get soccer out of your head? Then take some time out and do something else.
Remember – it's supposed to be about having fun!

MENTAL FITNESS

Soccer is fun, isn't it? That's how it should be and that's why you're playing the game.

The moment soccer stops being fun and becomes a chore, it's time to stop, think seriously and figure out what's gone wrong.

Maybe you are pushing yourself too hard. Maybe someone else – your coach, or a parent – is pushing you too hard. Maybe that someone is criticizing you too much, or not giving you enough praise for the good things you do.

Whatever the reason, you must remember that soccer is just a game, and having fun while you're playing it is more important than anything else – scoring a goal, making a great save, winning a match, or even winning an actual championship. Whatever anyone else tells you, it's only a game and it's there to be enjoyed.

Winning is not everything. Even pro players can gain enjoyment from a game they lose, and you'll find you're just the same. Although winning a game is a great feeling, it's really not that important to your life if you lose.

Some youngsters don't enjoy their soccer because they're scared – scared of losing, scared of what their coach or parents might say, scared of making mistakes. But don't worry: no one, not even the highest-paid pro, has ever ended a soccer match without having made a mistake or two. It's okay and completely natural to make mistakes, and you know what? It helps you to learn and improve your game as well.

No one with any sense is going to criticize you for making mistakes. Coaches and parents should be encouraging you, showing you the right way to do things, giving you praise when you get it right. If you take one lesson out of this book, then let it be this one: soccer is only a game, and it's a game that's played for fun.

INJURIES

Soccer is a physical game with a lot of contact. You wouldn't have it any other way, would you? Imagine the game without any tackling, struggling for possession of the ball or collisions between players. It just wouldn't be the same.

In any physical game, there is a risk of getting hurt. Luckily, injuries tend to be far less common in kids' football than in the adult game, but no one should go into a game of soccer without knowing the risks they are taking.

With younger players, soccer injuries are mostly little cuts, scrapes, bumps and bruises, but there's always the chance of something a little more serious.

Your coach should have some knowledge of basic first aid, and your team might be lucky in having some more experienced medics around, but it would do no harm at all if you picked up a little knowledge yourself.

So what should you or your coach do if you cut yourself on the field? If it's a minor cut or graze, you should clean the wound with water and pat it dry with a sterile dressing. If your coach is doing this, he should wear disposable gloves. Once the cut is clean, it can be covered with a dressing or plaster.

If the cut is more serious, your coach should apply pressure to the wound with a dressing, to stop the flow of blood, try to raise the body part above your heart and call the emergency services.

Pressure should also be applied if you have a nosebleed. Pinch your nose

It can be particularly hazardous for a goalkeeper

with your fingers until the bleeding stops and, if it doesn't, go see your family doctor.

Sprains and strains of muscles, tendons and ligaments are also quite common injuries on the soccer field.

Here, your coach or medic should be using the principle known as RICE, and encouraging you to visit the doctor as well.

RICE stands for Rest, Ice, Compression, Elevation, and is a good method of limiting the damage caused by injuries. The injured part should be rested, an ice pack applied to it to reduce swelling, compressed to cut down bleeding around the injury and elevated, again helping to reduce swelling.

More serious injuries, like broken bones and head injuries, sometimes happen on the soccer field, although they're very rare among younger players. These are the type of injuries that really should be left to medical professionals, once the adults on the scene have used their first aid training to do what they can.

The player here is about trip the other player up to attempt to get the ball – this could result in a red card and, worse still, a potential injury

A BRIEF HISTORY OF SOCCER

The Chinese military played a game using a leather ball way back in the second century BC

The phenomenon known as soccer, with its multi-millionaire stars and huge TV audiences, can be traced back to a game played in China over two thousand years ago.

Today, kids all over the world put down two sweaters to make a goal in the local park, while others take part in organized coaching schemes. But how many of them thank those Chinese pioneers for what Pelé called 'the beautiful game'?

The game played in the second and third centuries BC by the Chinese military was called tsu chu – 'kicking a ball'. Players aimed to kick a leather ball filled with feathers into a small net fixed on to bamboo canes. In another version, a player could use his feet, chest, back and shoulders to play the ball.

Later, the Japanese developed a game called kemari. The players stood in a circle and passed the ball to each other without letting it touch the ground. The ancient Greeks also had a soccer-type game, called episkyros, and the Romans had their own version, called harpastum. There were two teams, with a role assigned to each team member, a rectangular field and a center line.

But the sport as we know it today developed out of the Shrovetide matches played in the British Isles right up until the 19th century, often using an inflated pig's bladder as the ball. These medieval games were played under many different sets of rules. Each region had a different version of the game, which often featured vast mobs of players from neighboring villages. The object was often to carry the ball from one village to the next.

These violent matches sometimes resulted in serious injuries and even death, and the authorities often tried to ban them. The Lord Mayor of London was one of the first to try to ban soccer, way back in 1314.

The football pitch itself has been ever evolving – this diagram is taken from the 1930s

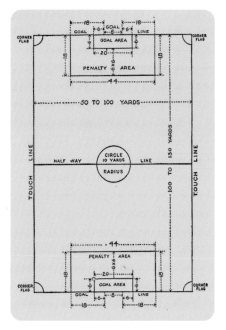

A more organized version of soccer, called calcio, was played in Florence, Italy, in the 16th century. The players often dressed in fine silk, but calcio was a violent pastime, with punching and kicking of opponents allowed. Back in Britain, the authorities were still doing their best to ban soccer, and in 1835 an Act of Parliament made it illegal to play the game on a public highway.

But things began to change as young men in British private schools started to show enthusiasm for the game. This is where the roots of modern soccer can be found, although each school had its own rules. Some schools allowed the ball to be carried; others favored a game in which skills such as dribbling were at the forefront.

American football's roots can be traced back to 1846 and a school in England

Someone needed to produce a standardized set of rules, and in 1846 Rugby School did just that, allowing handling of the ball and shin-kicking; here we see the beginnings of today's rugby football and American football.

But there was still confusion, and scholars at Cambridge University tried to produce a uniform set of rules. But it wasn't until 1863, when clubs and schools got together in London, that the modern sport began to take shape. Shin-kicking, tripping and ball-carrying were banned, 14 laws of the game were laid down, the rugby-playing men left to form their own union, and the Football Association was finally born.

It wasn't long before the FA had 50 member clubs, and the oldest soccer competition in the world – the Football Association Challenge Cup – was first contested in the 1871/72 season. The international face of modern soccer can thus be dated back to 1872, when England tied 0-0 with Scotland. Players were first paid seven years later, when Darwin town played

the amateur Old Etonians, and then professionalism was legalized in 1885.

Meanwhile, soccer was spreading all over the world. The Netherlands and Denmark formed football associations in 1889 and they were followed by countries such as New Zealand, Argentina, Chile, Switzerland, Belgium, Italy, Germany and Uruguay.

The United States was fairly slow in setting up a soccer body: the US Football Association (now the US Soccer Federation) was formed in 1913, nine years after the 1904 establishment of the world governing body FIFA (Fédération Internationale de Football Association).

The founders were Belgium, Denmark, France, the Netherlands, Spain, Sweden and Switzerland, but other nations soon flocked to join FIFA. By the time of the first World Cup in Uruguay in 1930, the federation had 41 members. Now there are well over 200 member associations from all over the world.

Players have gathered to contest the FIFA World Cup 17 times, and the tournament vies with the Olympic Games for the title of the world's greatest sporting event.

Today, just about every country in the world has some kind of soccer league structure, and countless numbers play the sport on a more informal basis. The millions who gathered in Germany for the 2006 World Cup probably had no idea they were part of a tradition that has its roots in ancient China and medieval English games played with a pig's bladder… but it's true.

The World Cup was originally called the Jules Rimet Trophy after the FIFA president who started the competition

INDEX